JACQUES RÉDA · TREADING LIGHTLY

Jacques Réda
Treading Lightly

SELECTED POEMS 1961–1975

Translated by
Jennie Feldman

ANVIL PRESS POETRY

Published in 2005
by Anvil Press Poetry Ltd
Neptune House 70 Royal Hill London SE10 8RF
www.anvilpresspoetry.com

French texts reproduced by permission of Gallimard
from *Amen. Récitatif. La tourne* (1988)
Copyright Editions Gallimard, Paris, 1988
Translations copyright © Jennie Feldman 2005

This book is published with financial assistance
from Arts Council England

Designed and set in Monotype Ehrhardt by Anvil
Printed at Alden Press Limited
Oxford and Northampton
ISBN 0 85646 380 9

A catalogue record for this book
is available from the British Library

ACKNOWLEDGEMENTS

Some of the translations in this collection, or earlier versions
of them, have appeared in *Agenda*, *Ambit*, *Lyric Poetry Review*,
Modern Poetry in Translation, *Poésie & Art*, *Poetry Review* and
Poetry Wales.

I am very grateful to Gabriel Levin, who first introduced
me to the work of Jacques Réda, for his thoughtful advice
and encouragement along the way. I would also like to thank
Stephen Romer for his helpful comments.

CONTENTS

Récitatif

La tourne

ON JACQUES RÉDA

IN THE JARDIN DU LUXEMBOURG with time to spare before our meeting, I'm reading my by now disintegrating copy of *Amen. Récitatif. La tourne*. No mistaking the "airy spring in the step that still makes firm contact with the ground even when ... it seems to free itself". The image could fit Jacques Réda's poems or person equally. In fact, though, it is his description of the inexhaustible appeal of jazz. Réda had made his name as a leading jazz critic long before he became one of France's major writers. For years an eminent figure in French-speaking literary circles in Europe and beyond, his transposition into English has been inexplicably scant. Individual poems have appeared in Anglophone journals and anthologies, but of his more than thirty books of poetry and prose, only one – *The Ruins of Paris*, a collection of prose poems – is available in an English version. D. Aspinwall's 1983 translation of *Récitatif* (IBP) is no longer in print.

Had Jacques Réda's work not been recommended by a French-speaking friend with well-stocked shelves, I might never have discovered this singular poet. Once discovered, his was a voice that I wanted, more than any other, to try and make heard in English. The elation of that first encounter on the page never left me. So now, some years on, here I am in the shade of flowering *marronniers* with a stack of draft versions, as Jacques Réda – tall, sturdy and, despite his more than seventy years, an "airy spring" in his step – joins me for a morning's work.

Amen. Récitatif. La tourne (Gallimard, 1988) combines in a single volume his first three major books of poems (1968, 1970 and 1975, respectively). Written during the period of experimental ferment in French literary circles that followed the demise of surrealism and engaged, political poetry,

9

these works anticipate the "new lyricism" that was to gather momentum in the 1980s. Réda was a key figure in this development. As editor of the prestigious *Nouvelle revue française* from 1987 to 1995, he was in a position to encourage new poets. Moreover the markedly realistic tone of his own work has been credited with helping to "ground" tendencies to lyrical flightiness. Indeed, in contrast to the abstract form of expression found in much modern French poetry, there is a sharp visual instinct at work throughout Réda's œuvre. It is interesting to note, in this connection, that he is an admirer – and translator – of Robert Frost, among other Anglophone poets. Many of his poems, he says, were generated by a single stubborn image of something seen or imagined: tokens of a Catholic childhood, a woman selling wool, reflections in a puddle. Some, like "October Morning", which came to him after reading a book on the Russian Revolution, are powerfully cinematic.

As we go through the drafts, his pen hovers, ready to sketch a translation where words fail. (Réda's skill as an illustrator is evident on the front cover of *Les Ruines de Paris*.) Already we have a pine slope in profile, a false-bottomed wine glass, a schematic map of Paris. And such is the visual imperative, that sometimes his pensive, modest manner gives way to exquisite and unselfconscious pantomime: Réda *élève* hunched over the furtive, furious scribble of youthful verse at his Jesuit boarding school ("where I first encountered serious literature – we had no books at home") or trying, unsuccessfully, to smuggle in unvetted volumes of poetry.

The passion for literature was later pursued independently of any university framework. Might this be a factor in the refreshing candour and wry self-doubt that characterize his writing? The list of literary influences he names is long, and somewhere near the top is the Geneva-born writer Charles-Albert Cingria (d. 1954), whom Réda extols, tellingly, for "his inventive and comic liberty of language, intelligence and vision". Others on the list include Theocritus, Ovid, Borges, Dante and Wordsworth, along-side the major French figures: Ronsard, Racine, La Fontaine, etc. He can quote hundreds of lines by heart. On request, he fluently delivers Virgil, du Bellay, Valéry, their sonorities lingering richly above our café table. This classical grounding is fundamental to his poetry, much of it written in lines of twelve syllables – the venerable Alexan-drine – or fourteen, and often rhymed. It is within, and against, these conventions that Réda deploys the originality of a true virtuoso. He makes the language dance, says poet and literary critic Jean-Michel Maulpoix, by playing on syl-lables like a pianist and by exploiting the rhythmic potential of the variable, "pneumatic" mute *e* at the end of French words. He also takes bracing, syncopating liberties with syntax, a practice that French tolerates better than English:

> *Mais sans nom prononçable est cette fosse qui sépare*
> *En deux l'être et, de chaque battement du cœur,*
> *Fait un choc de porte marquée après l'expulsion.*

("Hôtel Continental")

Réda has insisted that if (French) poetry is to survive, it will not be through conferences, confessions, "logoman-cies" or avant-garde eccentricities, but only by reclaiming that which distinguishes it from most prose, namely "rhythm, or better still, *le swing*". Swing and blues, he says, not least in their "airy" yet "grounded" aspect, have an existential value that calls on the affinities between music and language; this is an area often explored in his prose writings. In conversation once with a French *jazzophile* who reads all of Réda's jazz commentaries, I was told he has an uncanny, unrivalled ability to realize the sound of, say, Charlie Parker: in a couple of paragraphs, the music lifts off the page.

For a French writer, notes Réda, jazz cannot offer a *prosodic* model, as it might for a Kerouac or a Dylan Thomas. One can detect, however, a certain *jazziste* mode in his poems, which evolve in pensive riffs with unexpected asides and digressions, often in parentheses. A blues-y bittersweetness is played out in metaphors that blend intensity and insouciance, apprehension and bemusement: "... not suspecting it would be so / Terrible to give back this soul which acted / As if it had grown used to us".

Beside Réda's coffee-cup is the simple camera he keeps handy for any detail that might catch his eye during his long walks around Paris, a city he knows more intimately than most. A sharp observer of the everyday, he is also a seasoned practitioner of *flânerie*, that aimless, reflective strolling favoured by many city-dwelling writers and thinkers, Baudelaire and Walter Benjamin among them; poet-*flâneur* Jean Follain (d. 1971) occupies pride of place on Réda's list of mentors. Beyond Paris, he has roamed the country, on foot and on an antiquated Solex moped, from his native Lorraine to the Pyrenees and Provence. The musings and insights born of these wanderings have become something of a trademark. Through the *flâneur*'s shifting perspectives, urban, suburban and rural scenes, veering between consolation and menace, become expressive both of themselves and of his thoughts. At sunrise, "The day's equable rose already spiking through brambles" is observed above a gully with its "Bones, rusting iron, plastic, obscenities of the dead".

In his poems Réda's gaze is often fixed on the sky, which seems intimately connected with the creative process ("winter's limitless, fragile sky, / Where words' transparency is delicate as hoar-frost"). Being both absolute and changeable, remote and immediate, physical but also metaphysical, the sky engages dynamically with the poet's solitude. It expands hope or clamps a lid down, it dazes, looms, witnesses, is a continuity with other times and places; but it also – classic Réda – suffers disquiet: "Lost in its own immensity, uneasy space / Settles to a sky spread with grey".

Like space, time features as a pervasive aspect of consciousness; the pathos of our brief encounters with the eternal can be heard in the disabused, melancholic register – "our language / Where disaster sings an undertone" – that one also finds in the work of fellow poets Paul de Roux and Gilles Ortlieb. But "time in suspense", to quote Réda, is also an imaginative limbo in which light, in various gradations, holds sway:

> A single thread of silence where time shines
> In pensive brilliance like snow's first fall...
>
> ("Sky Slowly Approaching")

In *Ruines de Paris* we are told that despair does not exist for a walking man, as long as he's really walking and doesn't keep getting sidetracked into conversation. The *flâneur*'s equipoise between internal and external awareness, neither one dominant, each keeping the other in check, helps to explain the universal aspect of Réda's "je". Introspection is the re-angling of a lens that he also trains, no less quizzically, on wider human – and sometimes cosmological – vistas. He recognizes in himself, with characteristic self-deprecating wit, man's stubborn adherence to daily routine as a dignified response to the riddle of existence: "... knot your tie deftly to keep you safe from solitude and death". Solitude, bottom line of the human condition, is also the focus of poems dealing with ruptured love; *personified* solitude – in French, the word is feminine – variously shares the poet's evening meal, "[lifts] the soul a little in the broken light" or "takes her hand away from mine / And leaves me".

And what of mortality, that other bottom line of the human condition? On the one hand, awareness of it lies at the heart of a deep compassion for "my fellow travellers... / A convoy of shadows towards the deceptive light of day" – the train motif is a recurring one. But on the other hand, the prospect of death also provokes fascination, "Shrinking like a rounded breath / On the pane". What often strikes him, says Réda thoughtfully, is not that we must inevitably "disappear", but that we are *capable* of doing so. (And here our discussion is interrupted by a raucous flock of crows dropping into the tree beside us. Réda, ever responsive to such gifts, cocks an eyebrow: "Ah, c'est Hitchcock".)

In all his work, not least the new detective novel and even newer spy novel, there's a protean imagination conjuring scenarios that show an eye for detail and drama, but also a flexible diction that stretches to the metaphysical and the colloquial alike. In the poem "The Soul's Situation", reflections on the desire for eternity take in "the gods" who "Humbly order a toddy at the station bar / And throw up at daybreak against a tree". There are resonant apostrophes – "Lord of the bells' surging clamour" – but also down-to-earth locutions: "Enough's enough", from a mutinous follower of Moses; the homely "ma foi" mimicking an onlooker; "chouter", a verb borrowed from football slang. As the first line of an untitled poem explains, "What I wanted was to keep the words that are everyone's".

It has been remarked, not always kindly, that poets in France have a particular tendency to gather in cliques for mutual support. Réda, by contrast, though he has close literary friends, essentially walks alone. The years, it seems, have produced between the poet and the man an amiable compromise ("I am a bit asocial but quite sociable"), and also a sober realization: "Even if you are a poet all your life, it's mostly in the negative, in a state of expectation and anxiety". Never, though, without music. When he's walking, he says, he nearly always whistles or hums – anything from Potato Head Blues to liturgical melodies learnt as a boy. So there must be some tune in the air as, our meeting over and the goodbyes said, he heads off down the *allée*, a package for his grandson under one arm. "What is poetry after all", Jacques Réda has written, "if not life itself? One day goes well, another doesn't. To each his own little dancing step towards his limit, his god, his precipice".

JENNIE FELDMAN

PRÉFACE

De Paul Valéry, que j' ai beaucoup lu dans ma jeunesse
et pour qui je garde une affection et une admiration sans
doute tout à fait démodées, j'ai retenu entre autres une
remarque sur le *don* qu'est souvent pour son auteur le pre-
mier vers d'un poème qui, ensuite, exige une application
souvent plus proche de l'artisanat que de la griserie lyrique.
Ce premier vers n'est pas nécessairement celui qui com-
mencera le poème, mais celui qui en définit le *ton*, et avec
lequel le reste du poème, pour prendre corps, devra
demeurer en consonance. À tort ou à raison, l'auteur y
entend se manifester dans son propre système harmonique
une sorte d'écart et de nouveauté. Pour ainsi dire l'écho
d'une autre langue dans laquelle il lui faut transposer tout
ce qui – donné encore ou réfléchi – ne lui vient que dans
une tonalité habituelle. C'est en quoi le type d'activité
mentale qui caractérise l'élaboration d'un poème, évoque et
même préfigure celle qui absorbera l'auteur de sa véritable
traduction. Le plus simple est alors d'en rendre le mot à
mot aussi fidèlement et intelligemment que possible. Ne
méprisons pas ce parti. L'autre consiste en somme à
réécrire le poème originel après en avoir reconnu et saisi le
ton particulier, puis trouvé intuitivement son équivalent
dans la langue où il s'agit de le faire revivre. C'est une forme
de fidélité plus profonde, plus difficile, et qui suppose la
rencontre d'une sensibilité active et d'une expérience du
"métier". Il se peut que la réunion de ces qualités paraisse
moins surprenante chez une traductrice que de la part d'un
traducteur. Encore moins quand la traductrice a acquis
préalablement, dans sa langue propre, une rare familiarité
avec cette langue "autre" que font entendre universelle-
ment les poèmes, afin de nous rapatrier.

Jacques Réda

PREFACE

PAUL VALÉRY, whom I read a lot when young, and still – unfashionably, no doubt – hold in affectionate esteem, notes, as I remember, how a poem's first line is often, for its author, *le don*, the "gift" which then needs work that is often closer to craftsmanship than to lyrical rapture. That first line does not necessarily open the poem, but it does define the tone with which the rest of the poem must remain consonant in order to take shape. In that line the poet perceives, rightly or wrongly, something divergent and novel within his own system of harmonies. Some echo, as it were, of another language into which he must transpose everything – whether *donné* or thought out – that comes to him only in the usual tonality. It's in this respect that the kind of mental activity involved in working out a poem evokes, and indeed prefigures, the process that will engage whoever translates it truly. At its simplest, this means rendering the words as faithfully and intelligently as possible. Let's not underestimate this aspect. The other consists, in sum, of rewriting the original poem by first identifying and catching its particular tone, then intuitively finding the equivalent in the language where it is to be given new life. This form of fidelity is more profound and more difficult, needing both an alert sensibility and first-hand experience of the *métier*. Perhaps the convergence of these qualities comes as less of a surprise in a woman translator than in a man. Especially when she has already acquired, in her own language, a rare familiarity with that "other" language to which poems universally give voice, so as to repatriate us.

Amen

REBELLES

À la mémoire de Jacques Prevel.

COMME les fous ils ont mordu la terre à pleines dents,
Saisi l'herbe noire et coupante à poignées,
Jeté leur front contre le front des monuments
Qui méditent chez nous la mort et la justice.
Comme à des fous nous leur avons lié les mains et les chevilles,
Brûlé la langue et brisé les os sur les escaliers de justice,
Puis nous avons tassé la terre odorante et molle sur leurs
    fronts sanglants.
Ils sont paisibles maintenant; les plus menacés d'entre nous,
La nuit, parmi la foule des vieux morts les voient passer,
Tenant une sébile vide ou une crécelle, et leur bouche édentée
S'ouvrant pour un sourire où bascule notre sommeil.

REBELS

to the memory of Jacques Prevel

LIKE madmen they bit hard into the earth,
Grabbed the sharp black grass in fistfuls,
Dashed their heads one-to-one against monuments
That in these parts ponder death and justice.
Like madmen we bound them, hands and ankles,
Burned their tongues and broke their bones on the steps
    of justice,
Then we piled earth soft and fragrant on their bleeding
    brows.
They're at peace now; those of us who feel most threatened
See them pass by at night in the crowd of the long-dead,
Holding an empty bowl or a rattle, their toothless mouths
Opening for a smile that rocks our sleep.

FRONTALIERS

Bâtis pour abattre des arbres,
Tuer le porc ou broyer l'aviron,
Qui les a déroutés dès la lisière et faits lourds bûcherons
Dans la forêt d'allégorie où sont les bêtes véritables?
Horlogers en hiver, quand la vieille âme hercynienne
Par la combe toujours humide et noire brame
Vers la neige jonchée encor de célestes lambeaux,
Quel coffre ils ont,
Défricheurs mais hantés par la maison détruite
Et, dans ce décombre nocturne, à l'abandon:
Des petits au cul nu dont les mains ne seront plus jointes
Après la soupe, et comme il faisait bon;
Coffre d'os et de grosses bronches qui raclent
Entre la salamandre et le hibou, la hache
Vibrant dans la faille de chair du rien qui parle.

FRONTIERSMEN

Built to cut down trees,
Kill a pig or grind an oar,
Who misled them right at the forest edge, and made them
    heavy woodsmen
In the forest of allegory where real animals live?
Clockmakers in winter, when the old Hercynian soul
Bells out from coombes' perennial dark and damp
Towards the snow still strewn with wisps of sky,
What barrel-chests they have,
Squatters, but haunted by the wrecked house
And, in this night-time debris, adrift:
Bare-bottomed children who won't ever clasp their hands
    again
After the soup, and how good it was;
Chests where bones and huge bronchi rasp
Between the salamander and the owl, the axe
Vibrating in the cleft flesh of the nothing that speaks.

LA PORTE

ET POURTANT c'est ainsi: l'on voit, par la porte battante,
Une lumière qui s'approche, hésite puis s'éteint.
Souvent l'attente se prolonge. Et seul, à qui sourire
En silence? Personne. Et qui nous répondrait de loin
Si l'on criait? Personne encore. Un jour on croit rêver,
Un autre jour mourir – et vraiment c'est un songe, et c'est
Aussi la mort. Passent parfois deux lévriers timides
Et plutôt soucieux qui font mine d'en savoir long
Sur le sens de la vie. Incidemment, la porte cesse
De battre et l'on se dresse en criant plus fort dans le noir;
Ou bien la clarté s'établit, et l'on distingue enfin,
Pour un instant, ce qu'on ne peut pas dire ni comprendre.

THE DOOR

BUT STILL, this is how it is: you see, through the swing-
    door,
A light coming closer that wavers then goes out.
Often the waiting drags on. And who is there to smile at,
    alone
In silence? Nobody. And who would answer us from far off
If we shouted out? Nobody again. One day you think
    you're dreaming,
The next, dying – and it really is a dream, and it's
Also death. Sometimes two greyhounds come by, shy
And rather anxious, with an air of knowing all about
Life's meaning. Just then the door stops
Swinging and you're up shouting more loudly in the
    blackness;
Or else clarity sets in, and at last you make out,
For a moment, something you can't say or understand.

TRISTESSE D'HOMÈRE

CET HOMME ici devant la mer qu'il ne voit plus, un jour
Le direz-vous heureux comme celui du temps des dieux
Qui va s'effacer dans ma nuit?
                                    À l'aube dont je sens
Contre mes paupières vibrer la gloire, je descends
Vers ce miroitement obscur la ruelle autrefois
Rose, emportant le jour éteint dans les yeux de Patrocle
Et mon ombre en travers de la plaine étroite où le vent
Traîne le corps ensanglanté d'Hector dans la poussière.
À présent, songes, laissez-moi devenir tout entier
Cette ombre sur le vain éclat de nos débris d'amphores,
Et parmi ce fracas de boucliers sur les galets
Rendre ma voix à l'ïambe d'écume, aux cris d'oiseaux
Qui déchirent la belle hécatombe de mots que fut
Homère.
                    À l'étrave d'un vaisseau noir abandonné
Mon front s'appuie, et du sable au ciel noir mes doigts
    dessinent
Un signe pour toucher encor ta joue adorable,
                                                    soleil,
Mélancolie des morts.

HOMER'S SORROW

THIS man facing the sea, all sight of it gone now, will you
    one day
Say he's as happy as the other from the time of the gods
Who's about to fade into my night?
                              When dawn comes,
Its glory vibrant on my eyelids, I go down
The alley, once rose–pink, towards that dark sheen
Taking with me the daylight dimmed in Patroclus' eyes
And my shadow across the narrow plain where the wind
Drags the dust with Hector's blood-soaked body.
For now, dreams, let all of me become
This shadow on the hollow show of our ruined amphorae,
And in this clashing of shields on shingle
Give my voice to the foam's iambics, to the cries of birds
Tearing apart the fine hecatomb of words that was
Homer.
            Against the black prow of an abandoned vessel
I lean my forehead, and from sand to black sky my fingers
    trace
A sign wanting to touch once more your lovely cheek,
                                      sun,

Melancholy of the dead.

LA VOIX DANS L'INTERVALLE

PEUT-ÊTRE devons-nous parler encore un peu plus bas,
De sorte que nos voix soient un abri pour le silence;
Ne rien dire de plus que l'herbe en sa croissance
Et la ruche du sable sous le vent.
L'intervalle qui reste à nommer s'enténèbre, ainsi
Que le gué traversé par les rayons du soir, quand le courant
Monte jusqu'à la face en extase des arbres.
(Et déjà dans le bois l'obscur a tendu ses collets,
Les chemins égarés qui reviennent s'étranglent.)
Parler plus bas, sous la mélancolie et la colère,
Et même sans espoir d'être mieux entendus, si vraiment
Avec l'herbe et le vent nos voix peuvent donner asile
Au silence qui les consacre à son tour, imitant
Ce retrait du couchant comme un long baiser sur nos lèvres.

VOICE IN THE INTERVAL

PERHAPS we should speak even more softly,
So that silence can take refuge in our voices;
Saying no more than the grass as it grows
And the sand's droning under the wind.
Still without a name, the interval darkens
Like a ford when evening light slants over, and the current
Brims in an ecstasy of trees.
(And already the wood's gloom has turned up its collar,
Stray paths choking as they return.)
To speak more softly, under the sorrow and the anger,
Even without hope of being better heard, if it's true
That our voices like the grass and the wind can give
    sanctuary
To silence and in return be hallowed by it, miming
The way the sun declines as a lingering kiss on our lips.

MATIN D'OCTOBRE

Lev Davidovitch Bronstein agite sa barbiche, agite
Ses mains, sa chevelure hirsute; encore un peu, il va
Bondir de son gilet et perdre ses besicles d'érudit,
Lui qui parle aux marins de Cronstadt taillés dans le bois mal
Équarri de Finlande, et guère moins sensibles que
Les crosses des fusils qui font gicler la neige sale.
Il prêche, Lev Davidovitch, il s'époumone, alors
Que sur le plomb de la Néva lentement les tourelles
Du croiseur *Aurora* vers la façade obscure du
Palais d'Hiver se tournent.
                              Quel bagou; quel ciel jaune;
Quel poids d'histoire sur les ponts déserts où parfois ronfle
Une voiture aux ailes hérissées de baïonnettes.
À Smolny, cette nuit, les barbes ont poussé; les yeux,
Brûlés par le tabac et le filament des ampoules,
Chavirent, Petrograd, devant ton crépuscule, ton silence
Où là-bas, au milieu des Lettons appliqués et farouches,
Lev Davidovitch prophétise, exhorte, menace, tremble
Aussi de sentir la masse immobile des siècles
Basculer sans retour, comme les canons sur leur axe,
Au bord de ce matin d'octobre.
                              (Et déjà Vladimir
Ilitch en secret a rejoint la capitale; il dormira
Plus tard, également grimé, dans un cercueil de verre,

OCTOBER MORNING

LEV Davidovitch Bronstein ruffles his goatee, hands
    restless,
Ruffles his shaggy hair; in a moment he'll
Leap out of his waistcoat and lose his scholar's spectacles,
This figure addressing Kronstadt sailors hewn from the
    rough
Timber of Finland and with scarcely less feeling
Than the rifle butts that let fly dirty snow.
He preaches, Lev Davidovitch, he talks himself hoarse
    while
Over the leaden Neva the cruiser *Aurora* slowly
Turns its turrets towards the dim façade
Of the Winter Palace.
                              What a performer; what a yellow sky;
What a weight of history on the empty bridges where the
    odd car
Rumbles, its wings bristling with bayonets.
Tonight, at Smolny, beards have grown; seared
By tobacco and filament bulbs, eyes
Roll, Petrograd, before your twilight, your silence
Where out there, in an earnest crowd of grim-faced
    Latvians,
Lev Davidovitch prophesies, exhorts, threatens, trembles
Too as he feels the inert mass of centuries
Tilt irreversibly, like cannons on their axles
At the edge of this October morning.
                              (And already Vladimir
Ilitch is secretly back in the capital; later
He'll sleep, with the same dotard's make-up, in a glass
    coffin,

Immobile toujours sous les bouquets et les fanfares.
Cependant Lev Davidovitch agite sa tignasse,
Rattrape son lorgnon,
                              – un peu de sang, un peu de ciel
Mexicain s'y mélangeront le dernier jour, si loin
De toi boueux octobre délirant au vent des drapeaux rouges.)

Forever unmoving below the bouquets and fanfares.
Meanwhile Lev Davidovitch shakes his shock of hair,
Retrieves his eyeglasses,
                              – where a little blood, a little Mexican
Sky will mingle on the last day, so far
From you, muddy October, raving in the flurry of red
      flags.)

LE BRACELET PERDU

MAINTENANT je reviens en arrière avec vous,
Cherchant des yeux ce bracelet dans la poussière,
Par un midi si dur que la lumière semble
Elle-même se dévorer, bientôt absente
En son vaste brasier qui se volatilise.
                                    Et vous,
Qui vous agenouillez dans l'herbe blanche et les cailloux,
Votre profil, perdu sous l'horizon de vent qui nous entoure,
Fait de ce chemin creux une barque en dérive
Où nous serons ensemble à jamais maintenant,
Oubliés par le temps que la grandeur du jour immobilise,
Tandis que le sang bat à votre poignet nu.

THE LOST BRACELET

Now I turn and walk back with you,
Our eyes searching the dust for that bracelet,
Midday so harsh it seems the very light
Is being consumed and will soon be gone
As its vast brazier evaporates.
                                    And you,
On your knees amid the white grass and the pebbles,
Your profile, lost beneath the wind's horizon around us,
Turns this sunken road into a drifting boat
Where now we'll always be together,
As time, halted by the day's grandeur, forgets us,
And the blood pulses in your naked wrist.

APRÈS-MIDI

Pâle clarté d'après-midi sur les toits bleus et roses.
La cloche va sonner; on voudrait dormir comme l'arbre
À l'angle de la rue où ne passe jamais personne.
Mais l'astre d'insomnie est dressé là, strident
Comme un coq au milieu de la cour abandonnée,
Entre les timons dont le bois poli craint de luire.
Et tout ainsi, jusqu'à l'oiseau irréprochable qui s'est tu,
Frissonne dans la pauvreté humiliée des apparences.
Sommeil, ou mort, votre ombre est préférable à ce dévoilement
Infini des rêves livrés à l'ironie de la lumière,
Aux yeux qui n'ont plus de paupière et ne peuvent nier
Ce vide qui s'accroît soudain lorsque deux heures sonnent.

AFTERNOON

Afternoon's pale clarity above roofs of blue and rose.
The bell is about to strike; you want to sleep, like the tree
At the corner of the street where never a soul goes by.
But the orb of insomnia stands there, strident
As a cockerel in a deserted courtyard,
Between the shafts whose polished wood dares not shine.
And everything, even the blameless bird that's fallen silent,
Shivers in the humbled poverty of appearances.
Sleep, or death, better your shadow than this infinite
Unveiling of dreams laid bare to the irony of light,
Than eyes that no longer have lids and can't deny
This emptiness growing all of a sudden when the clock
     strikes two.

LENTE APPROCHE DU CIEL

C'EST LUI, ce ciel d'hiver illimité, fragile,
Où les mots ont la transparence et la délicatesse du givre,
Et la peau froide enfin son ancien parfum de forêt,
C'est lui qui nous contient, qui est notre exacte demeure.
Et nous posons des doigts plus fins sur l'horizon,
Dans la cendre bleue des villages.
Est-il un seul mur et sa mousse, un seul jardin,
Un seul fil du silence où le temps resplendit
Avec l'éclat méditatif de la première neige,
Est-il un seul caillou qui ne nous soient connus?
Ô juste courbure du ciel, tu réponds à nos cœurs
Qui parfois sont limpides. Alors,
Celle qui marche à pas légers derrière chaque haie
S'approche; elle est l'approche incessante de l'étendue,
Et sa douceur va nous saisir. Mais nous pouvons attendre,
Ici, dans la clarté qui déjà nous unit, enveloppés
De notre vie ainsi que d'une éblouissante fourrure.

SKY SLOWLY APPROACHING

THIS IS IT, winter's limitless, fragile sky,
Where words' transparency is delicate as hoar-frost,
And cold skin has its forest scent back again,
This is what contains us, being our true home.
And we set our lean fingers on the horizon
In the blue ash of villages.
Is there a single wall with its moss, a single garden,
A single thread of silence where time shines
In pensive brilliance like snow's first fall,
Is there a single pebble we do not know?
O perfect arch of sky, you answer our hearts
In their limpid moments. That's when
The figure treading lightly behind each hedge
Draws close; she is the far and wide coming ever closer
And her sweetness will take hold of us. But we can wait,
Here, in the brightness where already we're as one,
    wrapped
In our life as in a resplendent fur.

RUE ROUSSELET

DE LA RUE avec son vieux mur on dit qu'elle s'enfuit.
C'est vrai sur quelques pas après l'angle, puis tout s'apaise,
Et le vieux mur devient son propre reflet dans une eau
Très ancienne; et si l'on marchait, changerait-on de vie
Ou d'âme avant d'atteindre l'angle opposé qui navigue
En un temps différent, dans la lente clarté fragile
Des feuilles d'un jardin clos sur les souvenirs?
                                         La clé,
Nous l'avons vue un jour briller entre des livres, doigts,
Nuages oubliés; tous les rayons du soir la cherchent
Parmi la symétrie énigmatique des balcons
Où le ciel vacillant se penche pour attendre une ombre;
– Oblique à travers la douceur fugace de la rue,
Elle s'enfuit déjà par tout l'oblique de nos cœurs.

RUE ROUSSELET

THEY SAY the road with its old wall goes running off.
So it does, a few steps past the corner, then all grows still,
And the old wall becomes its own reflection in water
From long ago; and would you, if you walked on, change
    your life
Or your soul before reaching the opposite corner, which
    sails
By some other time, under the slow delicate light
Of leaves in a garden fenced around memories?
                                      We saw
The key one day shining between forgotten books, fingers,
Clouds; all the rays of evening are looking for it
In the enigmatic symmetry of balconies
Where sky leans over uncertain, waiting for a shadow;
– Slant against the road's fleeting loveliness,
Already it's slipping slantwise through our hearts.

FLAQUES

À PEINE un millimètre d'eau sous les arbres saisit
Le ciel convulsif qui s'apaise et qui s'approfondit
Pour que naissent entre nos pas l'hiver et ses nuages.
Et comme un inconnu surgi d'en haut notre visage
Apparaît un instant et sans rien dire nous sourit.
Oh répondez, ciel d'abîme innocent, bouche sagace,
Ouvrez-vous sans mesure avant
Qu'un peu de vent trouble à jamais l'espace dans l'eau mince.

PUDDLES

BARELY a millimetre's water under the trees, but it catches
Convulsions in a sky that eases and deepens
Letting winter and its clouds be born between our steps.
And like a stranger looming from above, our faces
Appear for an instant and saying nothing smile at us.
Oh answer, innocently fathomless sky, mouth of wisdom,
Open up immeasurably wide before
Some little breeze disturbs forever the space held in thin
    water.

AUTOMNE

AH JE LE reconnais, c'est déjà le souffle d'automne
Errant, qui du fond des forêts propage son tonnerre
En silence et désempare les vergers trop lourds;
Ce vent grave qui nous ressemble et parle notre langue
Où chante à mi-voix un désastre.
                             Offrons-lui le déclin
Des roses, le charroi d'odeurs qui verse lentement
Dans la vallée, et la strophe d'oiseaux qu'il dénoue
Au creux de la chaleur où nous avons dormi.
                                 Ce soir,
Longtemps fermé dans son éclat, le ciel grandi se détache,
Entraînant l'horizon de sa voile qui penche; et le bleu
Qui fut notre seuil coutumier s'éloigne à longues enjambées
Par les replis du val ouvert à la lecture de la pluie.

AUTUMN

AH, I KNOW that sound – autumn's wandering gust
Here already, breeding its thunder silently
Deep in forests and crippling overloaded orchards;
This solemn wind that's like us, speaking our language
Where disaster sings an undertone.
                              Let us offer him
The roses' waning, smells by the cartload slowly pouring
Through the valley, and the stanza of birds he unravels
In the warmth that cupped our sleep.
                              This evening's
Sky long shut within its brightness, expands and breaks
      away
Dragging the horizon of its slant sail; and the blue
That was our habitual threshold moves off in long strides
Through the creased vale lying open for the rain to read.

LA RENTRÉE

L'AIR d'automne est si clair qu'au-dessus de la ville
On entend craquer les forêts d'Alsace et de Lithuanie
Et passer des renards dont l'œil a la tendre sauvagerie
De ce ciel dénudé qui tremble au milieu de la rue.
Un barrage a cédé très haut dans les gorges du levant,
Libérant le bleu sans rumeur qui déborde les cheminées
Et, par la porte ouverte au cœur étouffant de septembre,
Voici le vent couleur d'averse du matin qui rentre
Avec son odeur de terrier, de bois mouillé, de gelée blanche,
Et sa stature d'autrefois dressée comme une promesse.
Je tends les bras dans ce retour de milliers d'ailes
Vers ce qui fut promis par la cloche aiguë du collège sous le
    brouillard,
Vers les anges dépossédés qui guidèrent mes pas parmi les
    bogues de l'allée,
Et la gloire d'octobre à genoux dans les feuilles mortes.

SUMMER OVER

THE AUTUMN air is so clear that above the town
You hear the forests creak in Alsace and Lithuania
And foxes going by, their eyes full of the tender savagery
Of this barren sky that trembles in the middle of the road.
High in the gorges of the east, a dam has burst
Releasing the soundless blue that overflows chimneys,
And deep into stifling September, here comes through the
    open door
A wind the colour of morning rainshowers
With its smell of burrows, damp wood and white frost,
And the stature it once had, upright as a promise.
Amid this return of thousands of wings my arms reach out
To what was promised by the sharp college bell beneath
    the fog,
To the dispossessed angels who guided my steps through
    chestnut-husks on the path,
And October's glory on its knees in the dead leaves.

PORTE D'AUTOMNE

PORTE d'automne, lente écluse entre les peupliers;
Cataractes de paix dans le bleu guerrier de l'été;
Souffle du haut vantail sur les gonds criants des forêts;
Espace enfin, démarrage de tout l'espace à travers un espace
     vrai,
Mais retour où criait le couvercle noir du plumier.
Et non,
Je ne cherche pas une enfance à tout jamais paralysée
Entre les figures indéchiffrables qui se retirent,
Mais le pays qui s'ouvrait librement au bord de la saison seule
     et dure.
Oh j'aimais le tilleul dans la cour étroite du boucher juif,
Et cette lumière tranchée à coups de sabre entre le parc et
     les casernes, mais
Ce qui s'élançait vers le ciel délivré de septembre
Déjà me rappelait.
          (Et quoi encore?
Ils ont tué
Pol Israël dit Salomon dans un wagon du camp d'Écrouves,
Sous le même ciel innocent jusqu'en Ukraine aux blés brûlés.
Et moi qui posais mes quarante sous sur le comptoir pour
     le pot-au-feu du samedi,
Je suis ici à murmurer la poésie d'octobre!
                 – Écoute,
Il fallait se taire plus tôt.
À présent tous ces mots voués à la transparence menteuse,

AT AUTUMN'S GATE

AT AUTUMN's gate, a slow sluicing between the poplars;
Stillness that cascades through the summer's martial blue;
A gust from the high lock-shaft over the forests' creaking
    hinges;
In a word, space, all of space setting off across a real space,
But going back, to the creak of the black-lidded pencil case.
And no,
I'm not looking for a childhood eternally frozen
Among inscrutable figures who draw away,
But the country that opened out freely at the edge of the
    lone, harsh season.
Oh I loved the lime tree in the narrow yard of the Jewish
    butcher,
And that light in sword-cut slices between the park and
    the barracks, but
Something leaping towards September's liberated sky
Even then reminded me.
                  (And what else?
They killed
Pol Israel, known as Salomon, in a cattle-car from the camp
    at Écrouves,
Under the same sky innocent all the way to Ukraine and
    its charred cornfields.
And I who used to put my forty sous on the counter for
    the Saturday hot-pot,
Here I am mumbling October poetry!
                        – Listen,
Best to have kept quiet before this.
Now, all these words pledging a sham transparency,

Que disent–ils, si l'eau que je suis, doucement déchirée,
Oppose sa froideur musicale au retour du navire
Où ils auront pris place à nouveau, les disparus?
Mais c'est ainsi: la saison seule et dure qui s'annonce
Est aussi l'ouverture aux pas dans la neige du loup
Qui n'a pas de pays, n'a pas de souvenirs, ne sait
Que sa faim obtuse inscrite dans l'ordre où je me risque.)

What is it they're saying, if the water that I am, softly torn
    apart,
Sets its cold music against the return of the ship
Where all who had disappeared are back on board?
But that's how it is: the lone, harsh season coming on
Will also introduce the snow-prints of the wolf
Who has no homeland, has no memories, knows only
Its mindless hunger inscribed in the order of things
    where I venture.)

LA TERRE QUI S'ÉLOIGNE

NOUS pouvons dire *ici,*
Douces briques sans fin recuites par le désert,
Furent Ninive et Babylon; mais la terre,
Quand elle aura comme un charbon sanglant dispersé dans
    le ciel
Nos os, nos codes et le soc des dernières charrues,
Qui dira, désignant cet orbe annulé dans l'espace,
Ici fut le nid appendu entre les branches du soleil,
Le feuillage de l'arbre de parole et sa racine
Arrachée et jetée au feu sans flamme de l'éther?
(Et déjà nous nous éloignons un peu dans le sifflement des
    fusées;
Du sas étroit, l'éclaireur des routes d'étoiles
Émerge, et de ses bras épais saisit la terre mère
Comme la tête d'un enfant perdu qui reparaît en songe –
Et nul n'a plus de voix, ni le rêve, ni le dormeur,
Ni la nuit véhémente qui les emporte.)

EARTH RECEDING

HERE, we can say,
Mellow bricks endlessly baked by the desert
Were Nineveh once and Babylon; but when earth
Has trailed across the sky like gory embers
Our bones, our codes, the last of the ploughshares,
Who will say, pointing to this voided globe in space,
Here's where the nest hung between the sun's branches,
The foliage of the tree of language and its root
Torn up and thrown in the ether's flameless fire?
(And already we're moving off in a hiss of rockets;
Out from the narrow chamber comes the scout who tracks
    the stars
And with his thick arms clasps mother earth
Like the head of a lost child who reappears in dreams –
And there's no voice left in the vision or the sleeper
Nor in the urgent night that sweeps them off.)

AMEN

Nul seigneur je n'appelle, et pas de clarté dans la nuit.
La mort qu'il me faudra contre moi, dans ma chair, prendre
    comme une femme,
Est la pierre d'humilité que je dois toucher en esprit,
Le degré le plus bas, la séparation intolérable
D'avec ce que je saisirai, terre ou main, dans l'abandon sans
    exemple de ce passage –
Et ce total renversement du ciel qu'on n'imagine pas.
Mais qu'il soit dit ici que j'accepte et ne demande rien
Pour prix d'une soumission qui porte en soi la récompense.
Et laquelle, et pourquoi, je ne sais point:
Où je m'agenouille il n'est foi ni orgueil, ni espérance,
Mais comme à travers l'œil qu'ouvre la lune sous la nuit,
Retour au paysage impalpable des origines,
Cendre embrassant la cendre et vent calme qui la bénit.

AMEN

No LORD do I appeal to, and no clarity in the night.
The death I will have to hold against me, in my flesh, like
    a woman,
Is the stone of humility I must in spirit touch,
The lowest rung, the unbearable separation
From whatever I'll clutch at, earth or hand, given over to
    that journey like no other –
And that total overturning of the sky, past imagining.
But let it be said here that I accept and ask for nothing
As payment for a submission that carries its own reward.
And what that is, and why, I do not know:
Where I kneel there is no faith or pride, nor hope,
But as through the eye that the moon opens under the
    night,
A return to the intangible land of origins,
Ash kissing ash as a calm wind gives its blessing.

Récitatif

MAUVAISE TÊTE

ALORS je leur ai dit:
La nuée au-dessus de l'arche, moi je ne l'ai jamais vue
Et traîner cette boîte vide à présent ça suffit.
Retranchez-moi si vous voulez, en tout cas moi je me
    retranche –
De vos fêtes, de vos émeutes quand les sauterelles
Se font rares ou l'eau saumâtre, et de l'apostasie
Aussi de bœuf en bœuf qui vous roule dans la poussière
Mais l'œil toujours en coin vers la base de la montagne
Où le Vieux cornu resurgit pour casser de l'ardoise
Et cracher la fumée d'orage par les oreilles.
Malheur, je leur ai dit,
Que le fil des roseaux d'Égypte n'ait pas tranché
Ses petits poings serrés sur une âme déjà remuante,
Et l'éternité plate du fleuve englouti
La première marche du temps rouvert par la Promesse.
Mais moi souvent parmi les froissements innombrables du
    songe,
Écoutant glisser la robe d'une princesse vers les lotus,
J'ai détourné ces pas qui déjà foulaient la pente de l'exode:
La noire extermination, les signes sanglants sur les portes,
La tranchée dans la mer comme un coup de vent par les blés.
Qu'est-ce que c'est que cette patrie, au-delà des cailloux,
Dont vous ne goûterez pas l'herbe, et quel autre
Canaan que la mort? Qui nous a séparés
Du sombre Nil d'oubli dont on ne connaît pas les sources?

REBEL

THEN I said to them:
Me, I've never seen it, the cloud above the Ark,
And dragging that empty box around, enough's enough.
Cut me off if you like, anyway I'm cutting myself off –
From your festivals, your riots when the locusts
Grow scarce or the water brackish, and also from your
      apostasy
With ox after ox rolling you in the dust
But always with one eye on the base of the mountain
Where the Old Man with horns looms up to smash tablets
And spew stormy vapours from his ears.
Worse luck, I told them,
That the sharp Egyptian reeds didn't cut
His little fists clenched upon a soul already stirring,
And the river's flat eternity swallow up
The first march of time reopened by the Promise.
But me, amid the countless rustlings of a dream,
Listening to the skimming robe of a princess heading for
      the lotus flowers,
I've often turned aside those steps even as they trod the
      slope of exodus:
The black extermination, the bloody signs on the doors,
The furrow in the sea like a gust of wind through
      cornfields.
What is this homeland, beyond the boulders,
Whose grasses you'll never taste, and what Canaan
Is there but death? Who separated us
From the dark Nile of forgetting, with its sources no one
      knows?

Voilà ce que j'ai dit.

Ils se regardent maintenant, pour savoir qui jettera la première
pierre.

J'ai pitié d'eux, pitié du berger solitaire qui les pousse

Comme son ombre à travers ce néant de sable et de siècles.

J'ai pitié mais j'ai peur aussi, je voudrais être ailleurs de toutes
mes forces.

That is what I said.
Now they are looking at each other, to see who will throw
    the first stone.
I pity them, pity the solitary shepherd who pushes them on
Like his shadow across this nothingness of sand and
    centuries.
I pity them but I'm also afraid, I wish with all my might
    I were somewhere else.

TERRE DES LIVRES

LONGTEMPS après l'arrachement des dernières fusées,
Dans les coins abrités des ruines de nos maisons
Pour veiller les milliards de morts les livres resteront
Tout seuls sur la planète.
Mais les yeux des milliards de mots qui lisaient dans les nôtres,
Cherchant à voir encore,
Feront-ils de leurs cils un souffle de forêt
Sur la terre à nouveau muette?
Autant demander si la mer se souviendra du battement de nos
    jambes; le vent,
D'Ulysse entrant nu dans le cercle des jeunes filles.
Ô belle au bois dormant,
La lumière aura fui comme s'abaisse une paupière,
Et le soleil ôtant son casque
Verra choir une larme entre ses pieds qui ne bougent plus.
Nul n'entendra le bâton aveugle du poète
Toucher le rebord de la pierre au seuil déserté,
Lui qui dans l'imparfait déjà heurte et nous a précédés
Quand nous étions encore à jouer sous vos yeux,
Incrédules étoiles.

EARTH'S BOOKS

LONG after the last rockets have ripped away,
Left in the sheltered corners of our ruined houses
To keep watch over the milliards of dead, books will be
All that remains on the planet.
But will the eyes of the milliards of words that used to
    read into ours,
Still trying to see,
Raise a forest breeze with their lashes
On an earth made mute again?
Why not ask if the sea will remember our legs kicking;
    the wind,
A naked Ulysses stepping into the circle of young girls.
O sleeping beauty,
Light will have fled like an eyelid closing,
And the sun as it lifts its helmet off
Will see a tear fall between feet that have ceased to move.
No one will hear the blind cane of the poet
Touch the stone's edge on the deserted threshold;
Already stumbling in the imperfect, he was there before us
While we were still at play under your eyes,
Unbelieving stars.

SITUATION DE L'ÂME

LA CHAIR, oui, mais l'âme n'a pas désir d'éternité,
Elle qui rétrécit comme un rond de buée
À la vitre et n'est que syncope
Dans la longue phrase du souffle expiré par les dieux.
Elle se sait mortelle et presque imaginaire
Et s'en réjouit en secret du cœur qui la tourmente.
Ainsi l'enfant que l'on empêche de jouer
Se dérobe les yeux baissés contre sa transparence.
Mais les dieux où sont-ils, les pauvres? – À la cave;
Et n'en remontent que la nuit, chercher dans la poubelle
De quoi manger un peu. Les dieux
Ont tourné au coin de la rue. Les dieux
Commandent humblement un grog à la buvette de la gare
Et vomissent au petit jour contre un arbre. Les dieux
Voudraient mourir. (Mais l'âme seule peut,
À distance des dieux et du corps anxieux
Dans son éternité d'azote et d'hydrogène,
À distance danser la mort légère.)

THE SOUL'S SITUATION

THE FLESH, yes, but the soul has no desire for eternity,
Shrinking like a rounded breath
On the pane, a mere syncope
In the lengthy phrase the gods breathe out.
It knows it is mortal and almost imaginary
And rejoices as such in secret away from the torturing
    heart.
It's how a child who is kept from playing
Slips away, eyes lowered against his own transparency.
But where are the gods, poor things? – In the cellar;
And they only come up at night, to look in the garbage
For a bit to eat. The gods
Have turned the corner on the street. The gods
Humbly order a toddy at the station bar
And throw up at daybreak against a tree. The gods
Would willingly die. (But only the soul can,
At a distance from the gods and the fretful body
In its eternity of nitrogen and hydrogen,
At a distance dance an airy death.)

LES LETTRES DE L'ÉPITAPHE

OH VIVRE ici, Démétrios, dans les bras repliés
Des collines. Avec un toit, du fromage, du vin,
Des fourrures de chèvre au lieu de casques sous la tête
Pour regarder le ciel à quoi nous ne comprenons rien
Couchés ce soir sur l'herbe rase où l'on a répandu
À l'aube les boyaux décevants d'une poule, où demain
Rouleront dans le sang tes drachmes au profil usé,
Mercenaire. Tu ronfles.
Peut-être qu'en dormant tu connais la forme des mondes
Et que nous en saurons la raison tout à l'heure
Quand la lumière ayant touché la pointe de nos armes
Il faudra y aller, camarade.
Noires sont les blessures au soleil qui a soif.
Que l'épée nous abrège: aucune immortelle, crois-moi,
Ne viendra salir ses pieds nus dans la sève de ceux qui gisent.
Empoigne donc la terre et mords, si tu veux qu'un peu de
        poussière
Ait pitié de ton ombre et se souvienne. En haut je ne vois pas
D'étoile qui déjà ne soit oubli, dur regard traversant
La fumée inutile des sacrifices.
Même les Infernales
Se taisent, et nous sommes seuls avec l'heure qui rétrécit.
Mais le ruisseau qui sépare nos feux de l'autre armée
En bas chuchote encore et fait luire entre les roseaux
Ces hautes tremblantes lettres que je ne sais pas lire.

LETTERS OF THE EPITAPH

OH TO LIVE here, Demetrios, in the folded arms
Of the hills. With a roof, some cheese, some wine,
Goatskins under our heads instead of helmets
To watch the sky where we don't understand a thing,
Stretched out this evening on cropped grass where at dawn
They spread a hen's disappointing entrails, where
    tomorrow
Your drachmas with their worn profiles will roll in blood,
Mercenary. You're snoring.
Perhaps in your sleep you can grasp the form of the worlds
And maybe we'll get the sense of them soon
When light touches the tip of our weapons
And off we must go, my friend.
Black are the wounds in a thirsting sun.
Let the sword keep us brief: believe me, not one of the
    immortals
Will come and dirty her bare feet in the sap of the fallen.
So grab a fistful of earth and bite, if you want a little dust
To take pity on your shadow and remember. Up there I
    don't see
A single star that hasn't already been forgotten, a hard
    gaze through
The useless smoke of sacrifices.
Even the Infernal Ones
Stay silent, and we are alone with the narrowing hour.
But the stream that comes between our fires and the other
    army below
Whispers on, and sets gleaming between the rushes
These tall trembling letters I cannot read.

LE CORRESPONDANT

Il arrive la nuit que je ne dorme pas durant des heures.
Autrefois je me retournais comme une folle dans mon lit.
Et puis je me suis mise à inventer des lettres
Pour des gens lointains et gentils, moi qui ne connais personne.
Maintenant je vois dans le noir, comme aux cinémas de
    campagne,
Des signes sur l'écran parmi des poussières d'étoiles:
C'est moi qui parle, ainsi qu'un champ de marguerites fleurit.
Si je voulais, je crois que je pourrais en faire un livre,
Et mes rêves aussi mériteraient d'être décrits:
Je descends de grands escaliers, en longue robe blanche;
Des personnes très bien m'attendent tout en bas des marches:
Ah nous avons reçu votre lettre, ma chère ... Il est minuit.
On s'éloigne en dansant sous les arbres qui s'illuminent.
Passent sans aucun bruit de profondes automobiles.
Les boulevards touchent le sable de la mer. Je ris,
Et c'est frais dans mon col de renard couleur de lune.
(Vous êtes là, ramassé sous le mur à l'ombre courte,
Comme au verger d'enfance où je n'ai pas osé pousser un cri.)

THE CORRESPONDENT

THERE ARE nights when I don't sleep for hours.
Once I would toss and turn like a madwoman in my bed.
And then I began to make up letters
For nice people in far-off places, I who don't know anyone.
Now I see in the blackness, as in out-of-town cinemas,
Signs on the screen amid the star-dust:
This is me speaking, like a field of daisies coming into
    bloom.
If I wanted, I think I could make a book of it,
And my dreams would be worth telling, too:
I come down great stairways in a long white dress;
At the foot of the steps distinguished company waits for
    me:
Ah we received your letter, my dear ... It is midnight.
Everyone goes dancing off under trees that light up.
Deep cars pass by noiselessly.
Boulevards graze the sand of the sea. I laugh,
And it's chilly in my fox-fur the colour of the moon.
(You are there, crouching by the wall with its bit of shade,
As in the childhood orchard where I didn't dare cry out.)

LA FÊTE EST FINIE

À Jean Ballard.

IL EST tard maintenant. Me voici comme chaque soir
Claquemuré dans la cuisine où bourdonne une mouche.
Sous l'abat-jour d'émail dont la clarté pauvre amalgame
Les ustensiles en désordre, un reflet dur écrase
Ma page confondue aux carreaux passés de la toile,
Et la fenêtre penche au travers de la nuit où tous
Les oiseaux se sont tus, et les mulots sinon les branches
Que le vent froisse et ploie, et les plis des rideaux,
Et les remous de l'eau contre les berges invisibles.

Mais qu'est-ce qui s'agite et crisse en moi, plume d'espoir
Qui s'émousse comme autrefois quand j'écrivais des lettres
Et que toujours plus flous des visages venaient sourire
En filigrane, exténués comme le sens des mots
Ordinaires: *tu sais la vie est plutôt difficile*
Depuis qu'Irène – ou bien *ne me laissez pas sans nouvelles*,
Et pour finir ces formules sans poids qui me navraient,
Ton père affectionné, ma grande, et tous ces *bons baisers*
Au goût de colle, de buvard et d'encre violette.

Non, soudain c'est ma propre image qui remonte et flotte
À la surface du papier, sous les fines réglures,
Comme le jour où chancelant sur le bord du ponton
Parmi les frissons du courant j'ai vu glisser en paix
Ma figure sans nom. – *L'identité du malheureux*
N'est pas avec certitude établie – oh laissez-le
Dériver; que son âme avec l'écume du barrage

THE FÊTE IS OVER

To Jean Ballard

IT'S LATE now. Here I am as every evening
Cooped up in the kitchen where a fly is buzzing round.
Beneath the enamel lampshade, its poor light amalgamating
Strewn utensils, there's a harsh gleam weighing down
My page, making it another faded square on the oilcloth,
And the window leans out into the night where all
The birds have fallen quiet, and the field-mice; only the
     branches
Jostled and bowed by the wind, and the billowing curtains
And swirls of water against unseen banks.

But what is this fitful rasping within me, hope's quill
Blunted as in the old days when I'd write letters
And faces ever hazier would come smiling
As a watermark, worn out like the meaning of everyday
Words: *you know life is rather difficult*
Since Irene – or else *don't forget to keep in touch*,
And ending with those empty phrases that grieved me,
Your affectionate father, *my big girl*, and all those *love and*
     kisses
Tasting of glue, blotting-paper and violet ink.

No, suddenly it's my own image that rises and floats
On the paper's surface, under the fine-ruled lines,
Like the day I stumbled at the edge of the landing-stage
And saw gliding peaceably amid the current's tremors
My nameless face. – *The identity of the victim*
Has not been finally established – oh let him
Drift; may his soul along with foam from the weir

Mousse encore, s'envole et vienne se tapir ici
Dans les fentes du plâtre et le grincement de la porte.

Alors comprendra-t-on pourquoi les jours se sont noyés
L'un après l'autre, jours divers, mais c'est toujours le même,
Hier, demain, jamais, qui réapparaît aujourd'hui
Et qui me voit rôder de la cuisine aux chambres vides
Locataire d'une mémoire où tout est démeublé,
Où jusque sous l'évier s'affaiblit l'odeur familière
Et, par les dimanches passés au rideau poussiéreux,
L'illusion que tout aurait pu de quelque autre manière
Conduire à d'autres seuils – mais la même ombre m'attendait.

Que reste-t-il dans les tiroirs: quelques cartes postales,
Deux tickets de bal, une bague et des photographies
Qui regardent au loin à travers de beiges fumées;
Plus pâles chaque jour ces nuages du souvenir
M'enveloppent, j'y dors sans poids, sans rêve, enseveli
Avec ce cœur docile et ponctuel qui fut le mien
Peut-être, et qu'emporte à présent le rythme de l'horloge
Vers le matin du dernier jour qui va recommencer,
Déjà vécu, levant encore en vain sa transparence.

Si doux, ce glissement du train de banlieue à l'aurore
(Quand de l'autre côté du carreau tremblant de buée
Le ciel vert et doré grandit sur la campagne humide)
Que c'est lui qui m'éveille aussi le dimanche et me mène

Turn to froth again, fly off and come to nestle here
In the plaster's cracks and the creaking of the door.

Then we'll understand why the days, each in turn,
Drowned, different days, though it's always the same one,
Yesterday, tomorrow, never, that reappears today
And sees me roaming from the kitchen to the empty
     bedrooms
Tenant of a memory where everything's been stripped,
Where even under the sink the familiar smell is fading
And, on Sundays spent behind a dusty curtain,
The illusion that everything, in some other way, could have
Led to other thresholds – but the same shadow awaited me.

What is left in the drawers: a few postcards,
Two dance tickets, a ring and some photographs
That gaze into the distance through beige mists;
Paler each day these clouds of memory
Envelop me, I sleep in them weightless, dreamless, buried
With this docile, punctual heart that was mine
Perhaps, and is now borne on by the rhythm of the clock
Towards the morning of the last day that will begin again,
Already lived through, raising its transparency once more
     in vain.

So pleasant, this gliding along at dawn in the suburban
     train
(When on the other side of the pane as it quivers with
     steam
Sky expands green and gold on the damp countryside)
That it's what wakes me on Sundays too and leads me

Jusqu'à l'enclos où j'ai mes tomates et mes tulipes.
Autour, dans la fumée et l'odeur aigre des journaux,
Songeant à d'autres fleurs, au toit de la tonnelle qui
S'effondre, mes voisins obscurs et taciturnes vont,
Convoi d'ombres vers la clarté menteuse du matin.

À cette heure malgré tant de déboires, tant d'années,
Je me retrouve aussi crédule et tendre sous l'écorce
Que celui qui m'accompagna, ce double juvénile
Dont je ne sais s'il fut mon père ou mon enfant, ce mort
Que je ne comprends plus, avec sa pelle à sable, avec
Sa bicyclette neuve, et son brassard blanc, son orgueil
Tranquille de vivant qui de jour en jour s'atténue
Entre les pages de l'album pour ne nous laisser plus
Que le goût d'une réciproque et lugubre imposture.

Muets, dépossédés, nous nous éloignons côte à côte,
Et ce couple brisé c'est moi: le gamin larmoyant
Que n'ont pas rebuté les coups de l'autre qui s'arrache
À la douceur d'avoir été, quand le pas se détraque
Et que l'on est si peu dans le faible clignotement
De l'âge, sac de peau grise flottant sur la carcasse
Déjà raide et froide où s'acharne, hargneuse, infatigable,
L'avidité d'avoir encore un jour, encore une heure
Avant de quitter le bonheur débile de survivre.

Ne pouvoir m'empêcher de songer à ma mort (si fort
Parfois qu'en pleine rue on doit le voir à ma démarche)
Alors qu'elle sera la fin d'un autre dont la vie

To the garden plot where I've got my tomatoes and tulips.
All around, amid the steam and the acrid smell of
    newspapers,
With their thoughts on other flowers, on the arbour roof
That's falling in, my fellow travellers go their way, obscure
    and taciturn,
A convoy of shadows towards the deceptive light of day.

At this hour, even after so many let-downs, so many years,
I find I'm just as tender and credulous under the hide
As that youthful counterpart who came with me,
My father or my child, I don't know which, that dead
    figure
I don't understand any more, with his beach spade, with
His new bicycle, his white communion arm-band, his quiet
Pride in being alive that every day grows weaker
Between the pages of the album, leaving us with no more
Than the taste of a reciprocal, dismal imposture.

Mute, dispossessed, we go off side by side,
And this ruptured couple is me: the tearful lad
Unfazed by blows from the other who tears himself away
From the sweetness of having existed, when steps falter
And we are so meagre in the faint blink
Of old age, a bag of grey skin floating on a carcass
Already stiff and cold, where the greed persists,
Nagging and tireless, for one more day, one more hour
Before quitting the feeble joy of surviving.

Unable to stop thinking about my death (so intently
Sometimes, people in the street must see it from the way
    I walk)
Though it'll be the end of someone else whose life

N'aura été que long apprentissage de la mort:
Pourquoi cette épouvante et ce sentiment d'injustice?
Qui te continuera, rêve d'emprunt d'où chacun sort
Comme il y vint, sans se douter que ce dût être si
Terrible de restituer cette âme qui faisait
Semblant de s'être accoutumée à nous? Je me souviens:

Un beau soir d'été dans la rue, est-ce qu'il souriait?
Voici qu'il tombe la face en avant sur le trottoir.
Autour de lui beaucoup de gens se rassemblent pour voir
Comment il va mourir, tout seul, attendant la voiture,
Se débattant pour la dernière fois avec son cœur
Et son âme soudain lointaine où subsiste un reflet
De l'improbable enfance, un arbre, un morceau de clôture,
Quelques soucis d'argent et peut-être un nom, un visage
Effacé mais qui fut l'unique et déchirant amour.

Et c'était moi qui m'en allais déjà; ce sera lui
Qui mourra de nouveau quand viendra mon tour; c'est
    toujours
Tout le monde qui meurt quand n'importe qui disparaît.
S'il me souvient d'un soir où j'ai cru vivre – ai-je vécu,
Ou qui rêve ici, qui dira si la fête a jamais
Battu son plein? Faut-il chercher la vérité plus bas
Que les branches des marronniers qui balayaient le square
Sous les lampions éteints, parmi les chaises renversées,
Quand le bal achevé nous rendit vides à la nuit?

Will have been no more than a long apprenticeship for
    death:
Why this horror and this sense of injustice?
Who will keep you going, borrowed dream from which
    each emerges
As he went in, not suspecting it would be so
Terrible to give back this soul which acted
As if it had grown used to us? I remember:

A fine summer evening in the street, was he smiling?
Now all at once he falls face down on the pavement.
Lots of people gather round to see
How he'll die, all alone, waiting for the ambulance,
Struggling for the last time with his heart
And his suddenly distant soul where a glimmer lives on
From improbable childhood, a tree, a bit of fence,
Some money problems and maybe a name, a face
Now faded that was the one and only, wrenching love.

And it was me already on my way; he'll be the one
Who dies again when my turn comes; it's always
Everybody who dies when anyone disappears.
If I remember an evening when I thought myself alive –
    did I live,
Or who's dreaming here, who will say if the fête was ever
In full swing? Must the truth be sought any lower
Than the chestnut branches sweeping the square
Under switched-off fairy lights, among the overturned
    chairs,
When the dancing was done and we were returned empty
    to the night?

Les fleurs que l'on coupa pour vos fronts endormis, jeunesses
Qui dansiez sans beaucoup de grâce au milieu de l'estrade
Au son rauque du haut-parleur, dans un nuage de
Jasmin, de mouches, de sueur, les yeux tout ronds devant
Les projecteurs cachés entre les frondaisons dolentes,
Les fleurs, las voyez comme en peu d'espace les fleurs ont
Glissé derrière la commode où leur pâle couronne
Sans musique tournoie avec les cochons du manège,
L'abat-jour en émail, les remous sombres du ponton.

Je ne revois que des cornets déchirés, des canettes
Dans l'herbe saccagée, et des guirlandes en lambeaux,
Et l'urne de la tombola brisée sous les tréteaux,
Et l'obscur espace du tir d'où plumes et bouquets
Ont chu dans la poussière. Et voici les objets perdus
Dans le tiroir que personne après moi n'ouvrira plus
Pour réclamer en vain cette lettre qui manque, mais
Pour rire d'un portrait de belle prise dans l'ovale
Et levant d'impuissantes mains jusqu'à son dur chignon.

Quel tenace et triste parfum d'oubli monte, s'attarde
Avec les cloches du matin qui rôdent sous les branches
Et la cadence de l'horloge au-dessus du réchaud.
Au loin dans le faubourg où finissent toutes les fêtes
Une dernière fois l'ivrogne embouche son clairon.
En bâillant, cheveux dénoués, la belle ôte ses bagues;
Au fond de l'insomnie où m'enferme le bruit des mots,
Son épaule de miel est-ce le jour qui recommence,
Son silence l'espace où vont éclater les oiseaux?

The flowers they cut for your sleeping brows, youngsters
Who danced without much grace mid-stage
To the raucous sound of the loudspeaker, in a cloud
Of jasmin, flies, sweat, wide-eyed in front of
Floodlights hidden in the long-suffering greenery,
The flowers, alas see how soon the flowers have
Slipped behind the chest of drawers where their pale circlet
Spins to no music along with the pigs on the merry-go-
    round,
The enamel lampshade, the dark eddies of the landing-
    stage.

All I see are torn wrappers, bottles
In the ransacked grass, and tattered garlands,
And the tombola tub in pieces under the stand,
And the dim shooting gallery where feathers and bouquets
Have fallen into the dust. And here are the lost things
In the drawer that after me no one will ever reopen
In a vain search for that missing letter, but only
To laugh at the oval portrait of a beauty
With hands raised helpless to her stern chignon.

What a sad, clinging scent rises out of forgetting, lingers
With the bells of morning as they roam under the branches
And the rhythm of the clock above the stove.
Far off in the suburb where all fêtes end
The drunk puts his bugle to his lips a last time.
Yawning, her hair loose, the beauty takes off her rings;
Deep in the insomnia where the noise of words encloses
    me,
Could her honey shoulder be another day beginning,
Her silence the space where birds will burst forth?

L'ŒIL CIRCULAIRE

CETTE horreur que mordent les dents entrouvertes des morts,
Eux l'avalent ensuite et demeurent en paix, lavés,
Les mains jointes sur l'estomac, commençant la glissade
Inverse par le démontage actif de la chimie.
Et leurs yeux qu'il faut clore d'autorité, jamais soumis,
Lâchent encore un regard sale et sage qui récuse,
Ayant vu, retourné comme un vêtement la lumière,
Et désormais rivé dans l'œil circulaire qui nous surveille.

THE CIRCULAR EYE

THIS horror the half-open teeth of the dead bite on
They will swallow and then be at peace, washed,
Hands clasped on stomach, as the sliding begins
In reverse through chemistry's active dismantling.
And their eyes that must be made to close, never
    submitting,
Still give a dirty, knowing look of objection,
Having seen, like something you wear, the light turned
    inside-out,
And from now on riveted in the circular eye watching us.

ORAISON DU MATIN

(OH MANQUE initial, et retrait dans l'élan comme d'une
    pelletée de cendres. Mais il y a lieu de se brosser les
    dents en fredonnant un air, et de nouer adroitement la
    cravate qui préserve de la solitude et de la mort.)

Jour, me voici comme un jardin ratissé qui s'élève
Tiré par les oiseaux. Fais que je prenne l'autobus
Avec calme; que j'allonge un pas sobre sur les trottoirs;
Que j'ourle dans mon coin ma juste part de couverture
Et réponde modestement aux questions qu'on me pose, afin
De n'effrayer personne. (Et cet accent de la province
Extérieure, on peut en rire aussi, comme du paysan
Qui rôde à l'écart des maisons sous sa grosse casquette,
Berger du pâturage sombre: agneaux ni brebis
Ne viennent boire à la fontaine expectative; il paît
La bête invisible du bois et le soleil lui-même
Au front bas dans sa cage de coudriers.)
                                     Mais jour
D'ici tonnant comme un boulevard circulaire
Contre les volets aveuglés qui tremblent, permets-moi
De suivre en paix ta courbe jusqu'au soir, quand s'ouvre
    l'embrasure
Et qu'à travers le ciel fendu selon la mince oblique de son
    ombre
Le passant anonyme et qui donne l'échelle voit
Paraître l'autre ciel, chanter les colosses de roses
Et le chœur de la profondeur horizontale qui s'accroît
Devant les palais émergés, sous les ruisselants arbres.

MORNING PRAYER

(OH THE LONGING at first, the impulse pulled back as
    from a shovelful of ashes. But it's as well to hum
    a tune as you brush your teeth, and knot your tie
    deftly to keep you safe from solitude and death.)

Day, here I am like a raked garden drawn
Upward by the birds. Let me take the bus
Calmly; step out soberly on pavements;
Hem my fair share of blanket in my corner
And give modest replies to the questions I'm asked, so as
Not to frighten anyone. (And this accent from the outlying
Province, it can also raise a laugh, like the peasant
Who roams well clear of houses under his bulky cap,
Shepherd of dim pastures: no lambs or ewes
Come to drink at the dawdling fountain; he grazes
The invisible beast of the woods and the sun itself
Sunken-browed in its cage of hazel trees.)
                                    But allow me,
Day, from here booming like a circular boulevard
Against the blind shutters' trembling,
To follow your curve in peace until evening, when the
    embrasure opens
And through a sky split in line with the thin slant of his
    shadow
An anonymous passer-by who sets the scale sees
The other sky appear, singing colossi of roses
And the choir of the deepening horizontal
In front of palaces coming into view, under streaming
    trees.

APARTÉ

MAIS le ciel, qui voudra l'ouvrir à l'ombre que je fus;
Et l'innocence de l'oubli, qui vous la donnera, mémoire,
Songes que la douceur n'a pu désaltérer, et toi
Sanglant désir rôdeur sous ce crâne d'ours?

ASIDE

BUT who will open heaven to the shadow that I was;
And who will give you, memory, the innocence of oblivion,
Dreams that tenderness could not quench, and you
Red-blooded desire prowling under this bear-skull?

PÂQUES

QUAND venait le printemps,
Fin avril l'air entier dans le parc déambulant
Comme une grande jeune femme en bleu marine et blanc
Dont on pouvait toucher la joue au détour des allées,
On allait acheter des sandales à petits trous,
Aux semelles qui boiraient l'eau de la première ondée,
Et le marchand donnait une image-réclame, avec
D'un côté les soleils de la crème Éclipse, de l'autre
Quatre dessins dont les replis d'arbres et de nuages
Cachaient les oreilles du loup et la taille de la bergère.

Cependant quelque chose de terrible avait eu lieu:
Peut-être les statues d'extase et de supplice
Avaient-elles saigné sous les ténèbres de leurs sacs
Et l'espace crié avant d'être englouti par l'espace
Où tremblaient au matin de fausses maisons, des petits arbres.

Seigneur de la clameur houleuse des cloches, dédicataire
Des blancs bouquets d'autel et des mains des petites filles
Levant leur couronne d'étoffe et leur âme de violette;
Dieu des accords fondamentaux quand l'être comme une perle
Brûlait entre les mains jointes sur leurs engelures
Et qu'à la porte de l'église en juin
La présence éclatante et sombre cherchait l'accès du cœur
    violent comme une torche –
Toujours ce ciel scellé sur la cour vide, et le murmure
Du robinet de cuivre au fond de la buanderie . . .

EASTER

WHEN spring came,
April over and all the air sauntering through the park
Like a tall young woman in navy blue and white
Whose cheek you could touch where the paths curved,
We'd go to buy sandals with tiny holes,
With soles that drank up the first rain shower,
And the shopkeeper would give out a picture leaflet with
Eclipse polish and its suns on one side, and on the other
Four drawings where folded trees and clouds
Hid the ears of the wolf and the trim shepherdess.

Meanwhile something terrible had taken place:
Perhaps the statues of ecstasy and torment
Had bled in the darkness of their bags
And space had cried out before being swallowed up by
    space
Where unreal houses and little trees trembled in the
    morning.

Lord of the bells' surging clamour, you to whom
White bouquets are dedicated at altars, and little girls'
    hands
Raising fabric crowns and the violets of their souls;
God of fundamental accords, when one's being would burn
Like a pearl between hands clasping their chilblains
And at the church door in June
The dark and dazzling presence would seek a way in to a
    heart violent as a flaming torch –
Always that sky sealing in the empty courtyard, and the
    murmur
Of the copper tap from inside the laundry ...

HÔTEL CONTINENTAL

LA SOLITUDE a justement ce nom doux et froid qu'on prononce
Et qui ramasse un peu l'âme dans la clarté rompue.
Alors de l'abandon et du retranchement surgit une figure
Qui fait signe à son tour sous les feuilles du papier peint,
Dans le grincement de l'armoire et les marges du livre
Illisible pour le regard qui de loin nous traverse.
Mais sans nom prononçable est cette fosse qui sépare
En deux l'être et, de chaque battement du cœur,
Fait un choc de porte marquée après l'expulsion.
Me voici maintenant au bord de la dernière marche,
Là où le réconfort naît de la présence d'une chaise
Et de la cavité murmurante du lavabo;
Où la main de la solitude elle-même s'est dessaisie
Et me laisse comme le jour où sous la pluie, après votre départ,
J'ai vu dans un cercle du temps qui n'est pas mesurable
Battre, fer contre fer, la petite porte du square.

HOTEL CONTINENTAL

SOLITUDE is chill and soft on the tongue that names it
Lifting the soul a little in the broken light.
Then out of the desertion and withdrawal a figure
Rises beckoning in its turn under the leafy wallpaper,
In the wardrobe's creak and the margins of a book
That can't be read by the distant gaze turned on us.
But there's no pronounceable name for this pit that divides
The self in two, and makes of every heartbeat
A slamming door with its eviction sign.
Here I am with one more stair to go,
Where consolation comes from a waiting chair
And the basin's hollow murmur;
Where even solitude takes her hand away from mine
And leaves me, like that day after you'd gone,
When standing in the rain I saw a circle of time
Impossible to reckon, and inside it
The little park gate clashing iron on iron.

BRUGES

À Michèle R.

JE N'AI PAS oublié non plus les petites maisons
De briques nettes, ni les jardinets à demi fous
Sur les canaux, ni la patience morte des femmes
Qui voudraient crier sous l'éclat du verre, des faïences
Et des meubles cirés jusqu'à l'usure de leur rêve
(Et le voici qui va tout seul dans l'épaisseur du chêne
Avec ces deux mains en avant qu'on ne reconnaît pas,
Ce corsage plus sombre où bat le cœur qui se dédouble),
Ni les ponceaux très bas, les pavés comme des genoux
Enfantins, le balancement de robe des allées
Sous le ciel énorme et trempé qui flotte, retenu
Par l'averse de soie et les attelages de cygnes.
Tant d'impasses où la mémoire ou le ciel de nouveau
Descend comme un regard lavé par les premières larmes,
Et l'herbe folle dénouée ainsi que des cheveux
S'écarte ô genoux bleus, linges que l'air soulève à peine
À l'appel étranglé dans la gorge contre le mur
Qui refait le compte avec soin de ses petites briques,
Les ressuie avec soin d'un peu de sang ou de salive,
Borne des cœurs cloués quand battent les ailes du rire
Le plus secret, l'écartelé, quand le temps marche d'or
Et d'ombre entre les ponts et se rue en silence au fond
Des chambres d'ombre et d'or et sans déchirer la dentelle.

BRUGES

To Michèle R.

NOR HAVE I forgotten the little houses, bricked
And spotless, the small gardens going wild
Along canals, or the deathly patience of women
Wanting to cry out under the lustre of glass, china
And furniture they've polished till the dream wore out
(And here comes the dream, walking alone in dense oaks
With these two outstretched, unfamiliar hands,
This darker bodice where beats a heart divided),
Nor the very low culverts, paving stones
Like childish knees, the skirted sway of avenues
Under an enormous sky, soaked and floating, held
In place by a silken shower and teams of swans.
So many dead-ends where again some memory or sky
Drops like a glance bathed in first-time tears,
And grasses wild and loose as untied hair
Spread wide, oh blue knees, linen the air
Barely lifts at the throat's strangled cry against the wall
That counts up its small bricks once more, carefully,
And carefully dries them of any blood or spit,
Furthest limit of pinned-down hearts when laughter
Of the most secret kind, torn apart, beats its wings,
When time moves on in light and shadow between
Bridges and hurls itself silently to the far end of rooms
In shadow and light and doesn't tear the lace.

FRAGMENT DES ÉTÉS

RIEN PAR l'immense été clos que le tremblement
Des rails sous les coquelicots, et la poule qui râle
Au fond de la chaleur noircissante; rien que
Ce duvet immobile et le nuage en exode, en fureur
Très lente sous la couvaison des préfectures, quand
Le destin surveillait les faubourgs par l'œil de la volaille
Augurale et figeait des trajectoires de céruse
Dans l'ocre à déchiffrer de la fiente par un enfant.
J'arrivais à la gare, je
Serrais frissonnant sous mon linge ce peu de glace
Et midi comme un poing d'aveugle sur les toits
Cherchait pour l'écraser ma tête transparente.
Mais loin sous les parois de l'œuf caniculaire
Je naissais de nouveau dans l'oubli, dans la pure fréquence
Que des ondes coupées des deux sources du temps,
Lambeaux d'une mémoire en détresse par tout l'espace,
Troublaient – et je voyais des morts, des femmes, des jardins
Me traverser tandis que vers le chœur du bleu marine
Entre les murs épiscopaux de Langres ou d'Autun
Je montais, et vers les jardins bouillant d'oiseaux et de racines
Enfouis dans la lumière ainsi que des yeux – et déjà
Sous les cils formidables de la chaleur n'était-ce pas
Les vôtres qui s'ouvraient en moi comme l'eau sous les cygnes?

FRAGMENT OF SUMMERS

NOTHING in all the vastness of high summer but the
    trembling
Of rails under poppies, and the hen's last rasp
From the depths of a blackening heat; nothing but
This quilted stillness and an exodus of cloud, furiously
Slow under the broodiness of prefectures, when
Fate watched over the suburbs through a fowl's
Auguring eye, and fixed trajectories of white-lead
In ochre for a child to interpret the droppings.
Arriving at the station, I
Would hold that bit of ice under my clothes
Shivering, and noon like a blind man's fist
Above the rooftops would seek out
My transparent head for crushing.
But far off, under the shell of a sultry egg,
I was born again into oblivion, into a pure frequency
Disrupted by waves cut off from time's two sources,
Shreds of a memory in distress all through space
– And I saw dead people, women, gardens
Pass through me as I rose towards the deep-blue choir
Between the episcopal walls of Langres or Autun,
Towards gardens that boiled with birds and roots
Sunken in light, like eyes – and even then
Under the heat's awesome lashes, were they not
Yours that opened in me like water beneath swans?

La tourne

Aussi j'entends sur le réchaud la berceuse du lait qui tourne.
Bon lait chaud d'autrefois je ne supporte plus, qu'il caille
Et crève sur le gaz étroit. Dors. Dors, laisse-le dire.
Inutile à présent de pleurer dans le téléphone,
Il n'en sortirait qu'un peu de fumée. Éteins et bois
Et va dormir dans la douceur de neige des limites,
Petite et toujours plus petite, et le jour diminue.
Entre les quatre murs aussi blancs que des ravisseurs
Qui n'espèrent plus, qui s'endorment,
Comme l'unique enfant de l'erreur et de l'amertume
La séparation est restée, elle oublie, elle joue
Avec une épingle, avec rien contre le plancher nu.
Et toi tu redescends la rue en cassant une plainte,
Et moi je la remonte en cherchant comment, pourquoi tu –
Si nous nous rencontrons qu'un vent sans pitié nous assomme.

AND ON the stove I hear the lullaby of milk turning sour.
Good hot milk from the past I can't stand any more, may
    it curdle
And perish on the narrow gas. Sleep now. Sleep, let it
    have its say.
No point now crying into the telephone,
All you'd get is a bit of steam. Switch off and drink
And go to sleep within bounds of a snowy softness
That's smaller and smaller, and the day draws in.
Between four walls white as kidnappers
Who have lost hope and fallen asleep,
Like the only child of error and bitterness
Separation stays on, forgets, plays
With a hairpin, with nothing, on the bare floor.
And you, you go back down the street hoarse with misery,
And I come back up it trying to figure why, how you –
If we meet, may a pitiless wind strike us down.

QUAND recommençait à briller le tilleul devenu si sombre,
  c'était la nuit
Et sous l'arbre non plus comme une bouche horrible (cette
  plainte
De bois sourd et d'oiseaux cherchant encore un morceau de
  lumière)
Mais la face d'argent d'un dieu tranquille qui protège,
À la proue ardente viraient l'étrave, les massifs,
Les hauts flancs constellés pour nos souffles: c'était la nuit;
La voix d'habitude si lente criait que l'heure était venue
Et vite qu'il fallait ranger si l'orage – l'orage
Dont luisaient presque tendrement les cornes dans l'impossible
Avenir appuyé déjà contre le mur encore chaud.

WHEN the lime tree that had grown so dark began to shine
    once more, it was night
And underneath, no longer like a monstrous mouth (that
    lament
Of dull wood and birds seeking another scrap of light)
But the silver face of a calm, protecting god,
The prow glowed as the bowsprit and massifs heaved
    round,
Tall slopes studded with stars for our breath: it was night;
The voice usually so unhurried was shouting the time had
    come
And quick, things had to be put away if the storm – the
    storm
Whose horns gleamed almost tenderly in the impossible
Future already leaning on the wall's lingering warmth.

DES FENÊTRES de l'hôpital on avait une vue
À vrai dire ma foi vraiment belle sur ces collines
Où des ifs et cyprès s'éparpillaient rythmiquement
Près du riant petit enclos de verdure et de marbre
Halte pour le soleil et peut-être vers le printemps
Deux ou trois promeneurs déjà dans la force de l'âge
Venant y méditer avec calme peut-être (non
Sur l'aboutissement hélas fatal de toute vie
Mais – des siècles ayant usé les dalles, consolant
Jusqu'à la douleur de garder un nom creux dans la pierre –
À la fin sur la mort de la mort elle-même et la
Douceur de bouger à jamais le pouce entre deux pages).
                                        Cependant
J'écoutais mon père à nouveau recommencer les comptes
        – emprunts, remboursements –
Lui quarante ans plus tôt qui d'une boîte d'allumettes
M'avait fait ce bateau resté dans les profonds courants,
Et si le croiseur noir venait aveugler la fenêtre
Y aurait-il me disais-je un espace le long des flancs
Pour cette barque afin qu'elle échappe vers l'étincelle
Qu'en me penchant un peu sur la gauche (n'écoutant plus
Mon père) je voyais dans l'œil obscurci de la baie?

FROM THE hospital windows there was a view
Really such a lovely view you know over those hills
And their rhythmic scattering of yews and cypresses
Near the pretty little enclosure with greenery and marble
A stopping-place for the sun and maybe towards spring
Two or three strollers already in their prime
Coming for some quiet reflection perhaps (not
On the fatal outcome alas of all life
But – where centuries had worn down the flagstones,
      keeping
The grievous consolation of a name hollowed in stone –
On the death of death itself in the end and the
Pleasure of sliding a thumb forever between two pages).
                                    But all the while
I'd be listening to my father go back over his calculations
      – loans, repayments –
He who forty years earlier had made me
This matchbox boat still upright in deep currents,
And if the black cruiser came blinding the window
Would there, I'd ask myself, be space alongside
For this vessel to slip away towards the spark
That leaning a bit to the left (no longer listening
To my father) I could see in the darkened eye of the bay?

ET JE REVOIS Janine au bout de cette barque étroite
Et laissant comme dans un film sa main filer sur l'eau
Son profil se pencher quand les fleuves pouvaient descendre
Et l'automne venir aussi ma liquide saison
Puisque les jours ne relisaient encore aucune trace
Et peu d'histoire dans le ciel d'été, retentissant
D'oiseaux et de bombardiers lourds souvent comme des
    brèmes,
Où mourir n'aurait eu de sens que pour d'autres, ce mot
Parmi d'autres parmi des fleurs et l'éclair des groseilles.
Et ma rame troublait à peine l'éternel le blanc
Non plus le blanc absolument de lis de sa culotte
Et de son cœur en sorte que tout seul la nuit venant
J'aimais l'absolu contre un mur entre l'œil froid de l'Ourse
Et la sourde consolation de l'eau nous emportant.

AND AGAIN I see Janine at the end of that narrow skiff
And she's trailing her hand on the water as in a film
Her profile leaning over when rivers could flow
And the autumn come my liquid season too
Because the days as yet read no sign
And not much history in the summer sky, resonant
With birds and bombers often as heavy as bream,
Where to die would have had no meaning except for others,
    that word
Among others among flowers and the flash of redcurrants.
And my oar barely ruffled the eternal white
Nor the absolute lily whiteness of her knickers
And her heart so that all alone with night coming in
I gave my love to the absolute against a wall between the
    cold eye of the Bear
And the dull consolation of water sweeping us on.

L'ÉCLAIR mauve passait dans les lobes énormes du gris
Et des bêtes broutaient sans bruit derrière l'églantine.
Trop blanc le blanc des fleurs dans le creux du jour assombri,
Noire noire la pluie en courant qui montait la colline.

Mauve lightning passed through the huge lobes of grey
And browsing cattle made no sound behind the dog-rose.
Too white flowers' white in the hollow of the darkened day,
Black black the running rain that climbed the hill.

JE REGARDE et je ne vois pas dans quel sens va le fleuve:
Trop de lueurs ou des ombres d'oiseaux pour me tromper
Entre les joncs où l'on entend des bêtes qui s'abreuvent
Aux flots épais comme du sang dont leur poil est trempé.
Elles rôdent le long des berges pour les défendre
Et je reste à distance avec des pierres dans les mains.
De l'autre côté de ce fleuve où je ne peux descendre
Un autre voyageur suit le même chemin.
J'ai perdu tout espoir d'une barque pour le rejoindre
Et nos gestes des bras par-dessus la gueule des chiens
S'espacent.

I'M LOOKING and can't see which way the river goes:
Too many glimmers or birds' shadows confusing me
Among the reeds where animals can be heard drinking
Water that courses thick as blood and soaks their fur.
They prowl along the banks defending them
And I keep a distance with handfuls of stones.
Across this river I can't get down to
There's another traveller following the same road.
I've lost all hope of a boat to take me to him
And our arm signals above the dogs' jaws
Grow distant.

IL Y AVAIT sans doute un remblai sur la droite:
La rue en contrebas, des lanternes de fer,
Un désarroi de rails sur les maisons étroites
Et le ciel plus immense et bousculé que si la mer
Battait dessous – la mer, l'égarement, l'angoisse
Quand le jour est définitif à quatre heures l'hiver
Et range doucement tout l'espace dans une boîte
Où l'on n'aura plus peur du ciel ni de la mer
Cassés comme les toits entre les distances qui boitent
Par les remblais et les couloirs et les rues de travers;
Où l'éclat sombre alors du sang dans la clarté si froide,
Sur la face des gens sortis en grand silence avec
De vrais gestes de fous qui voudraient encore se battre,
Perce (et l'instant d'après la nuit tombe, tout est couvert).

THERE WAS probably an embankment on the right:
The road leading down, iron lamps,
A confusion of rails above the narrow houses
And the sky more vast and tumbled than if the sea
Were thrashing below – the sea, the bewilderment, the
    anguish
When the day is final at four o'clock in winter
And gently puts all space into a box
Where there's no more being afraid of sky or sea
Broken up like the roofs between distances that limp away
Along embankments and passageways and side streets;
Where the dark gleam of blood in such chill light,
On the faces of people coming out quite silently with
All the gestures of lunatics who want to fight on,
Breaks through (and the next instant night falls, all is
    covered).

OR HUMBLE (connaissant qu'elle était la dernière)
Une lueur enfin libre de tout destin
Descendait les pentes d'ardoise vers les jardins
Et je me souvenais des soirs où la lumière
D'un bond s'arrache encore à l'abîme et l'on voit
Brûler contre l'angle d'un mur, au fond d'une fenêtre,
Les outils qu'elle pose avant de disparaître
Derrière les wagons de longs sombres convois
Où s'engouffrent bientôt ces foules sans parole
D'êtres indécis mais perdus et qui cachent leurs yeux
Sous des châles vraiment pénibles, sous de vieux
Chapeaux, tandis qu'un remuement d'eaux et de casseroles
Ronge au bas des talus la faible espérance des cieux.
Mais ce fut cette fois une lumière différente
Au visage enfoncé dans un renoncement profond
Et par l'obscurité devenue éclairante
Sans faste ni déclin dissipant ses rayons.
Et tout devant mes mains en repos sur la table
Comme les mains d'un autre encore dont j'entends
La montre – tout glissait avec un calme redoutable
Vers la clarté d'un jour sans ombre et délivré du temps.

NOW HUMBLY (knowing it was the last)
A gleam finally free from all destiny
Was coming down steep slates towards the gardens
And I was thinking back to evenings where the light
In one leap tears itself again from the abyss and you can see
Burning on the corner of a wall, in the depths of a window,
The tools it lays down before disappearing
Behind the carriages of long dark convoys
That will soon swallow up these wordless crowds
Of irresolute beings, lost nonetheless, who hide their eyes
Under really pitiful shawls, under old
Hats, while a stirring of waters and saucepans
At the foot of the slopes eats away the frail hope of heaven.
But this time it was a different light
With a face sunk in deep renunciation
And through the darkness becoming radiant
Scattering its beams without ceremony or decline.
And before me on the table my resting hands
Like the hands of someone else whose watch
I can hear – all gliding with formidable calm
Towards the clarity of a day without shadow and released
    from time.

À Michel Chaillou.

LA CONSTELLATION du Bélier couvre toute la plaine.
Son front plat, ses cornes de roc heurtent la poterne
Et font sauter à l'horizon des clous sur les dos ramassés
Des coteaux et des toits d'églises qui s'arc-boutent.
Entre deux tremblements des pattes
On voit se rétablir au fond de l'oreille spirale
La giration des astres lourds, des saints décapités.
C'est la roue, c'est la nuit. La fraîcheur
Court la cime de laine sur les forêts. Dessous,
Le vent pousse des doigts dans les chemins blancs en étoile,
Effleurant des troncs éblouis,
La perle en équilibre au bout des museaux qui hésitent.
Alors la maladie au creux de l'étang
Prononce avec douceur de très petites bulles
Et comme un bâton plongé droit, le regard
Du veilleur se brise en touchant la surface.

To Michel Chaillou

THE CONSTELLATION Aries covers the whole plain.
His flat forehead, his horns of rock butt the postern gate
And send nails flying to the horizon on the crouching backs
Of hills and church roofs braced foursquare.
Between a double trembling of legs
You see weighty stars' gyrations and headless saints
Resume their place deep in the spiral ear.
It's the wheel, it's the night. A coolness
Runs along the fleecy tops of forests. Below,
The wind thrusts fingers into white roads fanning out,
And lightly strokes dazzled trunks,
The pearl poised at the tip of wary muzzles.
Now the sickness deep in the pond
Softly mouths tiny bubbles
And like a stick held straight and dipped, the watcher's
Gaze, touching the surface, shatters.

JE MONTAIS le chemin quand j'ai vu d'un côté
Les sapins consternés qui descendent après l'office
Et de l'autre les oliviers en conversation grande
Fumant posément au soleil de toutes leurs racines.
Et droit sur les ravins à moitié remplis de bouteilles,
Os, ferraille, plastique, obscénité des morts,
La rose équitable du jour déjà crevait l'épine.
À chaque pas: le centre, et le cercle du temps autour
Bien rond mais moi j'étais autour aussi pour cette pie
Et pour d'autres chemins qu'il aurait fallu prendre, qui
    plongent
Vers des creux à l'affût, sous la viorne, de la folie.
C'est alors qu'il fait bon marcher avec du tabac dans la poche
Pour plus tard et chouter dans ces os et tôles sur les labours
Tandis que le soleil rame bas pour laisser tout le champ libre
    à sa lumière.

CLIMBING the road I saw on one side
Firs agitated on their way down from church,
And on the other, olive trees in grand conversation
Calmly smoking in the sun from every root.
And right above the gullies half-filled with bottles,
Bones, rusting iron, plastic, obscenities of the dead,
The day's equable rose already spiking through brambles.
At each step: the centre, and around it the circle of time
Curving, though I too am the curve for that magpie
And for other roads that should have been taken, that
	plunge
To the depths, lying in wait for madness under the
	viburnum.
That's when it's good to go walking with tobacco in your
	pocket
For later, and to kick through these bones and metal scraps
	on ploughed fields
While the sun rows low to leave the whole field free for
	its light.

À GAUCHE la rivière encore plus abstraite
Où pêchent des enfants dont les yeux réfléchis
M'intimident. Je continue à bicyclette
Vers le nord et le paysage s'élargit
Un peu trop: j'espérais des collines secrètes,
Des villages muets fourrés dans les replis,
Mais c'est toujours la plaine; au loin, de basses crêtes
Filent sous des poteaux. L'espace désempli
Dans son immensité s'égare, s'inquiète
Puis s'apaise en un ciel qui étale du gris.
Maïs et betterave. On ne voit pas de bêtes,
Aucun oiseau dans l'air, on n'entend pas un cri,
Et le temps même embarrassé de sa conquête
Somnole sans bouger derrière les taillis;
Mais sous l'arche d'un pont midi hâve me guette
Et j'entre dans son œil au diaphane iris.
Un talus croule ensuite avec des maisonnettes,
Des lessives en majesté sur les radis.
Les gens disent bonjour, d'autres baissent la tête
Qui fourgonnent sournois au fond des appentis.
Le chemin juste après subitement s'arrête
Contre un massif de ronce et de mauvais esprits:
J'y laisserais mes pneus, mon âme et ma casquette,
Il faut donc repasser devant ces gens surpris
(Malgré moi mon allure a cessé d'être honnête,
La lumière s'accroît de soupçons infinis
Et l'horizon du poids livide des tempêtes).

ON THE LEFT, the river more abstract still
Where children are fishing; their reflective eyes
Unnerve me. I keep on cycling
Northward and the landscape expands
A little too much: I'd hoped for secret hills,
Mute villages tucked in the folds,
But it's always the plain; in the distance, low crests
Run from post to post. Emptied out,
Lost in its own immensity, uneasy space
Settles to a sky spread with grey.
Maize and beetroot. No animals in sight,
Not a bird in the air, no cry to be heard,
And time itself perplexed by its conquest
Dozes unmoving behind the copses;
But under an arched bridge noon's haggard gaze
Follows me, and into its gauzy iris I go.
Next a tumbling slope with cottages,
Laundry majestic above the radishes.
People say hello, others bow their heads
And rummage furtively within their sheds.
A moment later the road suddenly halts
Against a mass of brambles and evil spirits:
That's where I'd leave my tyres, my soul and my helmet,
So I'll have to go back past those startled folk
(Somehow I've lost the honest look I had,
Light is growing with infinite suspicions,
The horizon bulked by the livid weight of storms).

Nous sommes trop à l'est et le soleil passe plus vite
Que sur les vergers du couchant ici quand le printemps
Déverse du sommet des montagnes toujours glacées
Des torrents de fraîcheur qui tourbillonnent dans les rues
Et détonent autour de brûlants piliers de parfums.
Le vent qui sur l'asphalte emporte une odeur de réglisse
Touche les corps avant de se glisser dans la chaleur
Étendue au fond du ravin. Alors il est sept heures,
Mais on voit s'embraser déjà les cargaisons d'étoiles
À travers le brouillard de l'herbe, et les lampes du pont,
Et les chiffres phosphorescents des montres. Les visages
Des gens précipités comme une avalanche là-haut
Brillent sans le savoir entre les banques qui s'éteignent,
Et par millions les pas se renfoncent dans le silence,
Dans la chaleur sous la géante étincelle des trams.

WE ARE TOO far east and the sun goes more quickly
Than over orchards to the west when spring here
Sends pouring down from the peaks of ice-bound
    mountains
Torrents of coolness that swirl in the streets
And explode around burning columns of fragrance.
The wind across asphalt carries a smell of liquorice
And grazes bodies before sliding into the warmth
Spread deep in the gully. Now it's seven o'clock,
But already through the mist off the grass you see
Cargoes of stars catching fire, and lamps on the bridge,
And the phosphorescent digits of watches. The faces
Of people rushing headlong like an avalanche high above
Shine without their knowing between closed banks going
    dark,
And footsteps by the million sink into the silence,
Into the heat beneath the giant spark of trams.

MAIS heureuse après tout fut la lenteur de ces journées,
L'heure en suspens comme une main sur l'épaule, compagne
Indifférente quand mes yeux s'ouvraient plus grands que moi
Pour sauver l'espérance inutile de la lumière.
Et quand au bas du ciel glissait la paupière violette,
De ce regard à demi clos je voyais resurgir
Méconnaissable dans la vitre obscure des boutiques
Une ombre à prendre en charge avec délicatesse, comme
L'étranger qui s'arrête et réclame du feu, sans un mot.

BUT happy after all was those days' slackness,
Time in suspense like a hand on the shoulder, a companion
Who didn't care when my eyes grew bigger than me
Wanting to save the vain hope of light.
And when the violet eyelid slipped low in the sky,
I saw rising again from that half-closed gaze,
Though barely recognizable in dark shop windows,
A shadow to be dealt with tactfully, like
The stranger who stops and wants a light, no word said.

Du côté de Schirmeck se pressent à pic par le brouillard
Les fûts autour d'une maison sans parois où le souffle
Demeure et rôde quand de rares mots passent les lèvres
Du marcheur pour se perdre au torrent qui ronfle plus bas.
Rien n'existe passé le bord hésitant de la route
Mais on sent l'altitude ronde et bien assise près
Du ciel qui dévale en fumant les flancs rouges d'aiguilles.
Grands fonts où les nuages font voile parmi les troncs,
L'abrupte et jamais baptisée au creux de sa hargne,
Du côté de Schirmeck, la terre s'y creuse encore
Et le cœur défoncé de paroles repose là.

TOWARDS Schirmeck tall trunks crowd steeply in mist
Around a house without walls where breath
Lingers and roams when a few words leave the lips
Of a passer-by and are lost in the torrent roaring below.
Nothing exists beyond the road's uncertain edge
But you feel the altitude rounded and steadfast abutting
The sky that rushes steaming down slopes red with needles.
Great fonts where clouds set sail amid the boles,
The abrupt and never-baptised earth entrenched
In its irritability, digs in deeper towards Schirmeck
And that's where the heart, stoved in by words, takes its
     rest.

CE QUE j'ai voulu c'est garder les mots de tout le monde;
Un passant parmi d'autres, puis: plus personne (sinon
Ce bâton d'aveugle qui sonde au fond toute mémoire)
Afin que chacun dise est-ce moi, oui, c'est moi qui parle –
Mais avec ce léger décalage de la musique
À jamais solitaire et distraite qui le traverse.

WHAT I wanted was to keep the words that are everyone's;
A passerby among others, then: nobody (unless it's
That blind-man's cane probing the depths of each memory)
So that anyone can say is it me, yes, it's me talking –
But with that slight variance in the music
Passing through him, forever on its own, abstracted.

DONC le temps est venu de les rassembler, tous les autres,
Tous ceux que j'ai perdus dans les coins obscurs de ma vie
Ou qui d'eux-mêmes détachant leur ombre de mon ombre
Attendent là butés sans comprendre ce qu'ils attendent
Contre un mur au fond d'une chambre où nul ne les saura.
Me voici devenu plus trouble qu'eux, bien trop étroit
Pour me diviser de nouveau; si faible,
Que remonter le flot qui s'étale, je ne peux pas.
Il faut pourtant les retrouver l'un après l'autre
Et les convaincre avec des mots précipités presque inaudibles
De me suivre: en bas au tournant je leur dirai pourquoi.
Mais le plus proche se détourne et ne veut pas m'entendre;
Il a peut-être peur de moi, peut-être tous les autres,
Sauf le plus lointain qui sourit, qui ne me connaît pas,
Et ses yeux d'espérance et d'oubli déjà m'effacent.

AND SO it's time to bring them together, all of them,
All those I've lost in the dark corners of my life
Or who themselves detached their shadow from my shadow
And wait there, not knowing why they're waiting, propped
Against the far wall of a room where no one will notice.
Here I am, by now more uneasy than they are, much too
    narrow
To divide myself up again; so weak,
That going against the broad current is beyond me.
Still I have to find them again one by one
And persuade them with a rush of words they'll barely hear
To follow me: down at the corner I'll tell them why.
But the nearest one turns away and doesn't want to listen;
Maybe he's afraid of me, maybe they all are,
Except for the one furthest off who's smiling, who doesn't
    know me,
His eyes with their hope and forgetfulness already blotting
    me out.

BRUSQUEMENT il se peut
Que l'un d'eux brusquement se dresse
Et rougisse, croyant qu'on l'a nommé.
Puis il s'apaise et considère sans bouger
Les chaises, les sureaux pressés entre la vitre
Et la glace du ciel qu'il voudrait voir tomber.
Et les voix de l'autre côté reviennent, restent prises
Dans l'épaisseur des murs appuyés à l'été
(Tout l'été au-dehors qui halète dans la poussière
Comme un grand chien noir, noir et bleu).

SUDDENLY it can happen
That one of them all of a sudden stands up
And blushes, thinking his name has been called.
Then he calms down and without moving contemplates
The chairs, the elder trees pressed between the pane
And the sky's glass that he'd like to see fall.
And the voices on the other side come back, held fast
In the thickness of walls leaning on summer
(All of summer outside panting in the dust
Like a great black dog, blue and black).

SORTIE un soir du soufflet crevé de l'accordéon
Elle vint entre les piliers de fonte du métro
Avec un grommellement de pauvre folle en savates
Et le blanc de son œil brillait moins que l'espoir douteux
Qui fait signe le long du square aux enfants qui s'échappent.
Elle ne m'a pas dit: *Eh, je suis la môme prière,*
Paye un verre au comptoir du boulevard Garibaldi —
Le haut comptoir sévère en zinc et bois mort où l'on paye
Comme avec des cailloux sur la lentille d'une mare.
Non, elle a fait grincer la porte et je n'osais pas boire
La gorgée obscure qui roule dans le double fond.
Des gens complètement fumés, paquets près d'une trappe,
Attendaient leur tour et déjà ne me regardaient plus
Et les vitres vibrant plus fort qu'un vieux train qui démarre
Je descendis en marche du bistro sans avoir bu.

EMERGING one night from the accordion's ruptured
    bellows
She came through the metal pillars of the metro
Mumbling like a crazed wretch in slippers
And the whites of her eyes had less shine than the dubious
    hope
That beckons to runaway children in public gardens.
She didn't say to me: *Hey, I'm the pick-up of your dreams,*
Buy me a drink at the bar on Boulevard Garibaldi –
The high bar with its forbidding zinc and dead wood
    where you pay
As with pebbles across the duckweed of a pond.
No, she made the door creak and I didn't dare drink
The mouthful swirling dark in the false-bottomed glass.
People thoroughly smoked, packages by a cellar door,
Were waiting their turn, by now no longer looking at me
And the windows shuddered more than an old train
    starting up,
The bistro on the move as I stepped down, my drink
    untouched.

PAUVRETÉ. L'homme assiste sa solitude.
Elle le lui rend bien. Ils partagent les œufs du soir.
Le litre jamais suffisant, un peu de fromage,
Et la femme paraît avec ses beaux yeux de divorce.
Alors l'autre que cherche-t-elle encore dans les placards,
N'ayant pas même une valise ni contre un mur
La jeune amitié des larmes? – Te voilà vieille,
Inutile avec tes mains qui ne troublent pas la poussière.
Laisse. Renonce à la surface. Espère
En la profondeur toujours indécise, dans le malheur
Coupable contre un mur et qui te parle, un soir,
Croyant parler à soi comme quand vous étiez ensemble.

POVERTY. The man gives his solitude some help.
She repays him well. They share the evening's eggs,
The litre that's never enough, a little cheese,
And the woman appears with her beautiful divorce-eyes.
So why does the other keep searching the cupboards,
When she hasn't even a suitcase or the youthful friendship
    of tears
Against a wall? – Here you are, an old woman now,
Not much use, with hands that don't disturb the dust.
Leave be. Give up the surface. Put your hope
In what stays deep and vague, in misfortune
Guilty against a wall, speaking to you one evening,
Thinking it's talking to itself, as when you were together.

L'APAISEMENT venu d'un coin du ciel qui s'éclaire, le queur
En caoutchouc reste percé d'aiguilles, ne saignant plus.
Il ressemble à du foie entre les plis de ta robe à toi, Vierge,
C'est-à-dire aplati rouge sombre et roulé dans la fine fleur.

WITH THE CALM that comes from a brightening corner
    of sky, the heart
Of rubber stays stuck with needles, the bleeding over.
It looks like a piece of liver in the folds of your own dress,
    Virgin,
I mean dark red, flattened and rolled in fine flour.

MON PARLER, c'est à vous que j'écris, à vous ma langue,
et j'ai douceur de ne pouvoir m'y prendre que par vous;
ma lettre pour vous parvenir ne franchit aucune distance,
entre vous et moi s'établit la correspondance immédiate d'un
amour enveloppant et tout à coup qui se déchire:
on voit la beauté violente des fleurs, les nuits sont dures,
les yeux difficiles à comprendre des filles deviennent
feuillage en transparence et ciel et terribles petites sources,
mais un vrai bond semble accompli dans la profusion réelle
et tu crois même ressaisir à pleines brassées
la vieille odeur de foin qui n'avait pas encore de nom,
o immer mehr entweichendes Begreifen,
o Angst, o Last, ô poids soulevé maintenant comme une plume,
o Tiefe ohne Grund maintenant traversée de rayons,
tu recommences mot à mot cette histoire muette
quand toussaient les chevaux des dragons au fond des écuries
et que rentrant à la maison tu voyais le temps pâle
entre les deux cris d'un oiseau qui ne volera plus.
Maintenant tu comprends,
maintenant le retour pas à pas s'explique:
une autre maison contenait celle où tu dormais contre ta mère,
une autre mère aussi veillait, chantonnant, tricotant,
ayant toujours à faire, à refaire, défaire (*le désordre est tenace*
le désordre toujours dès que l'on cesse de vouloir
se rétablit de lui-même avec grande facilité –
oh à mon tour déjà dans le souffle de la baleine

MY SPEAKING, it's to you I write, to you language of mine,
with the pleasure of knowing it's only through you that I can;
my letter covers no distance to reach you,
between you and me there's the instant correspondence of a
love that enfolds and suddenly rips apart:
one sees the violent beauty of flowers, nights are harsh,
girls' eyes that defy understanding become
leaves' transparency and sky and awful little watersprings,
but it seems there's been a true leap amid the profusion of
      what's real
and you even think you've recaptured in armfuls
the old scent of hay that didn't yet have a name,
o immer mehr entweichendes Begreifen,
o Angst, o Last, O weight lifted now like a feather,
o Tiefe ohne Grund now pierced with rays,
you start again word for word that silent story
when cavalry horses coughed inside their stables
and coming home you'd see time pallid
between the two cries of a bird that will fly no more.
Now you understand,
now the step by step return makes itself clear:
another house enclosed the one where you slept against
      your mother,
it was also another mother who'd keep watch, humming,
      knitting,
always with something to do, redo, undo (*chaos is persistent*
chaos always the moment you lose the will
takes over again by itself with the utmost ease –
oh my turn already in the breath of the whale

qui ne nous rendra plus sinon sur quel rivage où la
parole et le temps manquent comme une chute), ainsi donc
tricotant, chantonnant, allant, venant, venant
du haut du sommet enfoui, du fond de la couleur absente,
par cette lacune où devrait se fermer l'ogive du crâne,
dans la barque tirée entre les câbles du courant,
mais venant sans répit à petits craquements de branches
    mortes,
froissements d'herbe et gloussements sous la rive creusée,
tintements de cailloux sur la pente et partout contentement
circonspect et furtif du son innombrable qui monte encore
    maintenant dans sa naïveté première;
et puis toujours venant, venant, mais déjà divisée,
en route et sans cesse en route pour rassembler et disjoindre
    sur tous versants,
venant alors à petits gongs, petites clochettes, fous rires brefs,
    chapeaux pointus,
hing hing tch'ong hing hing,
à l'est à l'ouest au nord au sud au centre étendant son empire,
expulsant les montagnes, les fleurs, les oiseaux, les rivières
de leur certitude endormie et mettant à la place exactement
comme il vient d'être dit montagnes, fleurs, oiseaux, rivières,
mais pas longtemps, mais bientôt prise
de la peur affreuse d'une femme distraite et quand même un
    peu folle
qui dans une foule indifférente ne retrouve plus ses enfants,
qui les cherche, qui les appelle,
et sans doute est-ce plutôt la mémoire qu'elle a perdue,

that won't bring us back except to some shore where
speech and time are missing as in mid-fall), and so
knitting, humming, going, coming, coming
down from the hidden peak, from the depths of absent
 colour,
through that gap where the skull's arch should have closed,
in the ferry pulled between the current's ropes,
but coming on steadily with a slight cracking of dead
 branches,
grassy rustlings, a lapping under the scooped-out bank,
a ringing of pebbles on the slope and everywhere the
 cautious, stealthy
contentment of multitudinous sound now rising again in
 its primary innocence;
and then still coming, coming closer, but already divided,
on the move all the time on the move, merging and
 dispersing on every hillside,
coming now with little gongs, little bells, bursts of wild
 laughter, pointed hats,
hing hing tch'ong hing hing,
stretching its empire east west north south centre,
banishing mountains, flowers, birds, rivers
from their drowsy certainty and putting in their place
 exactly
as we've just said mountains, flowers, birds, rivers,
but not for long, but soon seized
with the horrible fear of a woman who's distracted, a bit
 crazy even
when her children go missing in a heedless crowd
and she looks for them, calls them,
when most likely it's rather her memory she's lost,

car elle ne sait même plus leurs noms, au hasard elle essaye
les syllabes les bruits qui clochent dans sa pauv'tête,
elle dit Kwiat, Kwiat, Fjellet, elle crie
Fuglen, Floden, Upe, Lumi,
Blomman, Kukka, Gorá, Zogu,
Rzeka, Madár, Ptak, Pták, Lintu,
et peut-être à la fin quelque chose ou quelqu'un va lui
    répondre,
mais en un sens on pourrait croire qu'elle s'en fout,
parmi les oiseaux et les fleurs elle traverse le temps, les
    montagnes, les cœurs, les rivières,
droite dans sa folie avec un sourire intérieur de patineuse à
    glace vraiment très forte qui repart en arrière,
et ceux qui parfois ont pu faire deux ou trois pas de cette valse
    à l'envers avec elle
(s'ils se souviennent,
s'ils n'ont pas tout lâché dans leur pantalon misérable entre
    les arbres disparus)
disent, ceux-là, qu'ils entendaient monter à travers le tonnerre
cette seule phrase Je suis parfaitement heureuse.

for she doesn't even know their names any more,
    randomly trying out
syllables, noises that clang in her poor ol' head,
she says Kwiat, Kwiat, Fjellet, she shouts
Fuglen, Floden, Upe, Lumi,
Blomman, Kukka, Gorá, Zogu,
Rzeka, Madár, Ptak, Pták, Lintu,
and maybe something or someone will finally answer her,
though in a sense you'd think she couldn't care less,
among birds and flowers she's passing through time,
    mountains, hearts, rivers,
erect in her madness with the inward smile of a really
    good ice-skater moving off backwards,
and those who have sometimes managed two or three steps
    of that reverse waltz with her
(if they remember,
if they haven't let it all out in their wretched trousers
    between the vanished trees)
it's those who say they could hear rising through the
    thunder
her single phrase, I am perfectly happy.